Other Titles Available
from Dorset House Publishing Co.

Becoming a Technical Leader: An Organic Problem-Solving Approach
by Gerald M. Weinberg

Data Structured Software Maintenance: The Warnier/Orr Approach
by David A. Higgins

Fundamental Concepts of Computer Science: Mathematical Foundations of Programming
by Leon S. Levy

General Principles of Systems Design
by Gerald M. Weinberg & Daniela Weinberg

Peopleware: Productive Projects and Teams
by Tom DeMarco & Timothy Lister

Practical Project Management: Restoring Quality to DP Projects and Systems
by Meilir Page-Jones

Rethinking Systems Analysis & Design
by Gerald M. Weinberg

The Secrets of Consulting: A Guide to Giving & Getting Advice Successfully
by Gerald M. Weinberg

Software Productivity
by Harlan D. Mills

Strategies for Real-Time System Specification
by Derek J. Hatley & Imtiaz A. Pirbhai

Understanding

Understanding the Professional Programmer

Gerald M. Weinberg

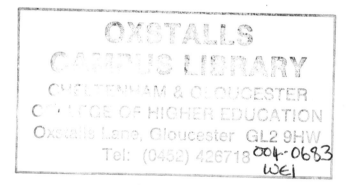

Dorset House Publishing, 353 W. 12th St., New York, N.Y. 10014

To the person in the title

Library of Congress Cataloging-in-Publication Data

Weinberg, Gerald M.
    Understanding the professional programmer / by Gerald M. Weinberg.
      p. cm.
    Reprint. Originally published: Boston : Little, Brown, c1982.
    Bibliography: p.
    Includes index.
    ISBN 0-932633-09-9 : $20.00 (est.)
    1. Electronic data processing personnel.   2. Computer programmers.
I. Title.
QA76.25.W45 1988
005.1'023'73—dc19   88-5098
                                                  CIP

Credits:

Pages 19–24, 42–43: Extracts reprinted by permission of Jo Edkins.
Page 143, Figure 3: From "In Search of Definite Statistical 'Proof' " by Gerald M. Weinberg from *Datalink*, October 1, 1979. Reprinted by permission of the publisher.

Pages 197–199, Figures 4, 5, and 6: From *General Principles of Systems Design* by Gerald M. Weinberg and Daniela Weinberg. Copyright © 1988 by Gerald M. Weinberg and Daniela Weinberg. Reprinted by permission.

Cover Design: Jeff Faville, Faville Graphics

Copyright © 1988 by Gerald M. Weinberg. Published by Dorset House Publishing Co., Inc., 353 West 12th Street, New York, NY 10014.

Hardcover edition was previously published by Little, Brown & Co. © 1982.

Portions of this book appear in *Becoming a Technical Leader, The Secrets of Consulting, Rethinking Systems Analysis & Design*, and *General Principles of Systems Design*.

Printed in the United States of America

Library of Congress Catalog Number 88-5098
ISBN: 0-932633-09-9

Foreword

In 1944, when I was eleven, I read a *Time* magazine article about computers! At that age, my mind was a clean slate looking for a piece of chalk, so the article made a great impression. I recall sitting in the high wing-backed chair in the living room, *Time* in my lap and time on my hands, deciding that I was going to become a "computer person." Much has happened to computers since 1944. Much has happened to our lives because of computers—especially to my life. But one thing, at least, hasn't changed. It's a lifetime later, and now I'm writing the computer articles instead of reading them. Yet even today nobody understands what "computer people" are, what they really do, and what they ought to be doing.

I shouldn't say that nobody knows. The problem is that *everybody* knows—but everybody knows something different. After a lifetime of computing, the dust still hasn't settled. Computer people still have the freedom to *choose* what they might do—and with it the freedom to choose what computers might do. Perhaps in another fifty or one hundred years, computer people will be slotted into rigid pigeonholes for life, but today our fate still seems to be in our own hands.

The computing business until now has depended on the free flow of ideas. In the old days you could go to a meeting once a month and talk to at least one person from every important installation in, say, Los Angeles. Now some old-timers go to the NCC and try to reestablish that old environment among 75,000 people from all over the world. But it's not the same.

And it will never be the same. What we once accomplished

naturally, by some sort of lemming instinct, now has to be accomplished by more explicit structures. For instance, at big meetings there's no room for little ideas. And at little meetings there's no room for the little shot, who's come to hear what pearls of wisdom the big shots might cast.

In the past, we depended on meetings because little was written down. When I started working for IBM in 1956, I read *every* piece of technical literature (including the entire SHARE library) in the San Francisco branch office in less than one week! That was pretty much all the technical literature IBM had in 1956.

Today, we are so swamped with technical literature that we have little time for face-to-face exchanges and seemingly no time at all for "informal" reading. So computer people everywhere are losing contact with one another, losing the flow of ideas that are too little or not sufficiently technical to put in manuals or textbooks. In doing so, we're losing contact with a significant portion of our reality, and our work suffers.

I sense this loss of contact most strongly when I read the letters from readers of my regular columns—*Stateside, Phase 2,* and *From Eagle, Nebraska.* There are computer people in Dubuque, Dublin, and Dunedin who share so much but who will never have the opportunity to meet face to face. If they did meet, they would instantly recognize one another as "computer people"—just as they have recognized themselves in these essays. What do I mean by a "computer person"? I mean the kind of person who reads these essays and says now and then, "Yes, I do that," or "I feel that way," or "I wish my manager understood that," or "I can use that technique," or even "This guy Weinberg has lost touch with the kind of environment *I* work in."

This series, then, is for people who want a better understanding of computer people—programmers, analysts, managers, designers, trainers, testers, maintainers, operators, administrators, architects, chiefs, or whatever they're called. I've tried to make the essays interesting, so as not to waste any of the very scarce reading time of the average computer person. You can pick up one of these books whenever you have five minutes to spare (like while you're waiting for TSO to respond), open it at random, and read a complete idea. It may not be the world's greatest idea, but it's all there and it might do some good. And if not, it might give you some pleasure—which will do some good in its own way.

Preface

The word *professional* carries several well-defined meanings as well as a heavy baggage of implications. To give the reader a better definition of the scope of this book, I'd like to explore which of those meanings I intend in my title.

My *American Heritage Dictionary* says that *professional* means "of, related to, engaged in, or suitable for a profession," which only throws the meaning back on the definition of *profession*. This would lead us into arguments of whether programming is a profession, whether it should be, and how it is to become one. I do not intend to engage the reader in these arguments in this book, though no doubt many of the essays here will throw some light or shadow on the subject.

The second and third definitions emphasize the receipt of pay for work. The professional programmer, in the sense I intend, probably receives pay for programming work, but not necessarily. Moreover, there are many who receive pay for programming work who I would *not* regard as professionals, for reasons that will become clear to those who read these essays.

The closest definition to my meaning of *professional* is this: *Having great skill or experience in a particular field of activity.*

This book is about the people who have great skill or experience in computer programming.

Unlike my earlier book, *The Psychology of Computer Programming*, this book does not attempt to encompass all the activities subsumed under the title "programming." The focus here is on the skilled and experienced performer—how to become one and how to remain one in a treacherous environment.

My old friend and adversary Phil Kraft took me to task for the title *The Psychology of Computer Programming*. As I understand his argument, there is no such thing, literally, as the psychology of an activity, but only the psychology of a person or persons. Phil may be happier with *Understanding the Professional Programmer* as a title (though I suspect he'll be enraged by some of the contents). I have emphasized the individual person in this title because the individual is the focus of the book.

Primarily, *Understanding the Professional Programmer* is intended as an exercise in self-examination for the professional programmer. A very wise counselor, Eugene Kennedy, says:

> Some persons examine themselves rather harshly out of motives that are a mixture of fearfulness and a need not to be found wanting. It is not difficult to raise guilt feelings in people, as most preachers and fund-raisers know. . . . Raising unnecessary guilt gives self-examination a bad name and may be the reason that many people shun it or postpone it and, therefore, never realize its values.

It's not my intention to raise guilt feelings among professional programmers. Quite the contrary; I believe that programmers have suffered too much from being the conventional and convenient target of a trade press primarily concerned with peddling hardware. To the least thoughtful journalists, programmers are merely an impediment to ever greater hardware sales and advertising revenues.

My point of view here is well described by Kennedy when he goes on to say:

> There is another way to look at ourselves; it is more the way a professional does it—whether a doctor or an athlete—accepting the need for a particular discipline in view of freeing the self for a steadily improving performance. It is part, in other words, of what healthy professionals do, not to punish but to improve themselves.

If you'd like to be a professional programmer in this sense, then *Understanding the Professional Programmer* is written especially for you.

Acknowledgments

I wish to thank the following colleagues whose correspondence has been quoted in this book: David Coan, Jo Edkins, Bob Finkenaur, David Flint, D. A. Martin, and Barbara Walker. I also wish to thank the many other correspondents who inspired me but who could not be directly identified.

I am especially grateful to those colleagues who read and ranked the many essays I considered for inclusion. Their comments and suggestions demonstrate once again how important reviews are to creative work. My "panel of experts" consisted of Jim Fleming, Mason C. Gibson, Tim Gill, Bill Hetzel, Roger House, Bob Marcus, and Paul Mellick. I couldn't have done it without them.

Nor could I have done it without my local panel of experts, Dani and Judy, who are never afraid to bring me back down to earth.

Contents

IV. Is It Possible to Think More Effectively?   91

V. Why Doesn't Everyone Understand Me?   121

VI. How Can I Survive in a Bureaucracy?   157

VII. Where Is the Programming Profession Going Next?   189

Part I

What Questions Are Important to the Professional?

How Long Does It Take
to Make a Programmer?

There are some subjects on which everyone is an expert. Teaching is a good example. Anyone with an IQ over 80 and knowledge of some subject or other is supposed to be able to teach. At least that's the theory on which the American university system is founded. In the United States, a professor is insulted, outraged, and likely to start legal action at the mere suggestion that *anybody* in the world could show him anything that could improve his classroom teaching.

Also in the United States, everyone is an expert on the subject of waiting tables. A European waiter may train for ten or twenty years before being allowed to serve in a first-class restaurant. In America, you become a waiter by answering an advertisement and putting a towel over your forearm.

Programming is another subject with no shortage of experts. Six weeks of "training" is typically considered all that is necessary to elevate one to the "expert" level, beyond the need for learning anything new and qualified to design on-line life-support systems. When you see an advertisement for "experienced" programmers, it often means about *one year* or perhaps two years of experience. Indeed, anyone with fifteen years in programming is considered some sort of mental midget. If he had the least bit of intelligence, he would have learned all there was to know about programming fourteen years ago. After that, he would have become so bored he would have sought a place in management or sales.

Yet before we go too far in ridiculing those who hold this view, we ought to acknowledge that fifteen years of experience, in and of itself, need not teach you *anything* about programming. I know American waiters who have fifteen years of "experience" and don't know how to set a plate on the table in front of the diner. And I know American college professors with fifteen years of "experience" who couldn't teach a dog how to wag its tail. Similarly, I know some American programmers with fifteen years of "experience" who still sort the transaction file before updating the direct-access master file in a multiprogrammed system.

Just in case that last example is too subtle, let me list a few items I found in one day, reading the programs of "experienced" programmers:

1. Someone who didn't know what a *remainder* was when using integer division!
2. Someone who converted a variable with range 0–5 to a variable with range 1–6 (for FORTRAN subscripting) using five IF statements and five assignment statements!
3. Someone who didn't use ELSE clauses in COBOL programs because "they don't always work."
4. Someone who never uses VARYING strings in PL/I because "they aren't efficient."
5. Someone who doesn't use subroutines at all because "they're too complicated."

The list could be extended indefinitely. The point is not merely that there are people out there passing as professional programmers who shame us all, but that *few managers have any way of telling if they're talking to one of them or one of us.*

It's very much like the situation with waiters in the United States. Very few people in the United States have ever been served a meal by a professional waiter, so they have no way of knowing one when they see one. Or, rather, they have no way of knowing that the typical waiter is subprofessional.

Similarly, there are very few ways of measuring the quality of a programmer's work unless you are a competent programmer yourself. There are many installations in the world that have *never* had a really competent programmer who stayed around long enough to establish a set of professional expectations. Each installation drifts into its own standard of mediocrity. These standards differ quite widely from place to place and even from group to group within a single installation.

When I go to a new organization to begin consulting, I ask the managers to give me, in advance, some *typical code*. Usually they cannot believe that I really want to see code, and I must insist several times before getting anything. From a small sample of code I am usually able to form a pretty accurate picture of the environment in the shop. Sometimes I can make marvelously specific predictions, so striking that the management thinks I've secretly been talking to some of the employees.

The managers themselves *never* look at code. Code is to programming managers what dirty dishes are to a headwaiter. Once you have graduated from the garbage heap, you *never* touch the garbage again—even in jest.

Once, while at college, we students suggested a Master's examination procedure that involved the professors' taking the same examination as the students, to establish qualifying standards. More than two-thirds of the professors recoiled in genuine horror. After subjecting themselves to the humiliation of examinations for twenty years, they were not about to return to a position that even *suggested* their former lowly status.

This attitude in our business suggests that writing code has a place in the hierarchy of human worth somewhere above grave robbing and beneath managing. It's not possible, to this way of thinking, that writing code might be a separate skill, or talent, or profession, with a ranking all its own—not measurable on the same scale with grave robbing and managing. As long as this attitude prevails in a data-processing environment, there will be six-week programming experts and managers who don't listen to their highly paid fifteen-year programmers.

What is it that teaching, waiting tables, and programming have in common? What makes everyone believe they can do these things as well as a professional? First, the work *seems* understandable, because it has been experienced by many ordinary people. Everyone has taught somebody *something*. Everybody has carried a platter to the table or helped clear away the dirty dishes. But not everybody has done surgery on a living brain, or argued a case before a jury.

But what of programming? Surely, not everyone has written a program, have they? Not everyone, perhaps, but just about every manager, accountant, engineer, or other university-educated professional has. Programming courses have become all the rage in universities and they are required in many professional curricula. IBM, for example, has, for the past twenty years, given executive seminars that include some "programming experience."

I don't know the present content of IBM's executive seminars, but for many years the seminars included the famous "Manhattan Problem" as the one and only programming exercise. For those of you who are culturally deprived, I'll repeat the Manhattan problem as printed in the most popular introductory DP textbook in the United States:

> The problem is to determine how much the $24 supposedly paid for Manhattan island in 1627 would be worth today if it had been placed in a savings account at 4½ percent annual interest.

(If 4½ percent seems a bit low, that's because the problem has been used since 1956 at least and has been copied by one generation of textbook writers after another.)

The "solution" to this problem, eliminating some inessentials, is the following FORTRAN loop:

```
  I = 1627
  PRINC = 24.00
2 PRINC = PRINC*1.045
  I = I + 1
  IF (I − IYEAR) 2,1,1
1 WRITE (3,601) PRINC
```

This "solution" has been taught to at least 3 or 4 million students, from executives to college freshmen. For many, it is the one and only program they have ever "written," but it qualifies them to judge the difficulty of programming an operating system, a labor distribution, a parts requirement plan simulator, an on-line process controller, or just about anything you can name. And, of course, in the executive courses, the students are given a professional assistant, "to help with the details."

Actually, the Manhattan problem *could* be an excellent vehicle for teaching executives the most important lesson they need to know about the programming profession. Suppose they are allowed to compose this little gem and to accept it as the "solution" to the problem. You then show them how much time it took to write, and how much time it took to execute, and ask them how "good" they think those figures are.

Once they have committed themselves, you show them that the same result could be obtained from a program reading:

```
PRINC = 24.00*(1.045**(IYEAR-1627))
WRITE (3,601) PRINC
```

You compare programming time and execution time. Depending on circumstances, you might find that the program takes 1/5 the effort and 1/100 the execution time. Then you ask, "If the most trivial problem imaginable can be programmed in two ways that differ in cost by factors of 5 or 100, what must the difference be between a professional and an amateur job of programming an operating system?"

With that sort of lesson, a programming literacy or appreciation course might be made to do more good than harm. As it now stands, the principal lesson of these courses, although never explicitly stated, is this: "Programming isn't so hard. With a few weeks of practice, even I could become an expert programmer."

Somehow, if programming is ever to be treated as a profession, the public—and the programmers themselves—will have to be educated. They must realize that even fifteen years will not suffice to complete one's knowledge of programming—unless one has a very closed mind.

Can the Handicapped Succeed as Programmers?

Whenever the market for programming talent becomes a seller's market, buyers attempt to broaden their source of supply. Hardened, grizzly old managers, when confronted by recent graduates demanding trainee salaries above the managerial scale, begin to interview women. Anglo-Saxon, Protestant managers turn to people whose skin isn't splotchy pink and whose church isn't even pronounceable. And robust managers who climbed the first three rungs of success on the football field start asking me whether it's "safe" to "hire the handicapped."

It's easy to get annoyed at the privileged classes when they display ignorance of the deprived classes. ("*Under*privileged" is a euphemism of the privileged which I can't bear to use in this context.) It's also easy to pick up the banner of the obviously deprived, knowing that nobody dare question your righteousness. On the other hand, if you speak of "hiring the handicapped" in strictly business terms, rather than in terms of the "social responsibility of the business community," you expose yourself to accusations of crass commercialism and lack of feeling. Nevertheless, I would like to attempt a rational approach to the issue of handicapped programmers. If this type of treatment offends you, you will probably make a poor employer of handicapped persons or at least of persons you label "handicapped."

Handicapped is, in the end, a label—a state of mind rather than a state of being. This point of view may be unfamiliar, so let me give a few examples of the performance of handicapped people in a field outside of programming, namely, sports.

One night we watched the televised story of a Czech pistol champion who lost his right arm in World War II, which we'd all agree is a handicap to a right-handed shooter. But this man's identification with pistol competition ran a bit deeper than his arm, so he taught himself to shoot with his left arm. And proceeded to win a gold medal!

Another television feature told the story of Wilma Rudolph, the American sprinter. When she was small, she was so sickly it was declared that she would never walk. I don't remember how many Olympic gold medals she ultimately won, but it was several more than you or I have won, and nobody ever told *me* I'd never be able to walk.

Of course, that story may simply say something about the state of American medicine, an idea that's reinforced by the performance of the former record holder in the mile, who had polio as a child and was also told he'd never walk. (On the other hand, American football has recently been graced by several top kicking specialists who had congenitally deformed feet, amputated toes, and in one case an artificial leg; so perhaps American medicine isn't so bad after all.)

Actually, I doubt that any of these stories have anything to do with medicine, but they do have a lot to do with hiring the handicapped. From these and other stories, and from watching the performance of blind, deaf, paraplegic, quadriplegic, and various handicapped programmers, I've concluded that success is in the mind, not in the eyes, ears, arms, or legs. When the handicapped person decides to prove to the world that she's no different from other people, she often overcompensates and becomes a champion, in programming as easily as in running.

To me, this ability to surmount a seemingly insurmountable handicap tells an important story. To be a champion kicker requires about one hundred parts motivation to every one part leg. The leg, after all, can be trained, but what do we know about training motivation? We know that if we amputate a few toes, we might produce a strongly motivated kicker, but are we willing to go that far? Are you willing to remove part of your brain just to become a better programmer? If so, you're probably blessed with sufficient motivation already, so you can skip the surgery.

Think about the programmers you know. How many of them seem to have all the blessings, all the raw materials of brain and brawn, yet never seem to rise above mediocrity? What would you do to make them realize how blessed they are? For most of us, we have to lose our blessings before we can count them.

Personally, I always took my hands for granted until arthritis made even electric typing painful. I used to complain a lot about it—what a terrific handicap for a writer—until I met a programmer who didn't have hands. I didn't even have to *try* typing with a stylus strapped to my head.

In programming, there's a particular kind of handicap that seems impossible to overcome, no matter how motivated one might be. I'm speaking, naturally, of the lack of intelligence necessary to do the programmer's job. Certainly, I'm not saying that low intelligence is a state of mind—or am I? Yes, I'll freely admit that there are some people in the world who haven't the intelligence to be computer programmers, if only because they haven't the intelligence to understand what a computer or a programmer is. But I don't think that's nearly as large a population as most readers might imagine.

Programming a computer does require intelligence. Indeed, it requires so much intelligence that nobody really does it very well. Sure, some programmers are better than others, but we all bump and crash around like overgrown infants. Why? Because programming computers is *by far* the hardest intellectual task that human beings have ever tried to do. Ever.

Depending on your religious persuasion, you may believe that human beings were (1) designed to swing from limb to limb eating bananas; (2) designed to live in the Garden of Eden eating apples; or (3) not designed for anything at all. Nobody's religion, to my knowledge, says that human beings were designed to write computer programs that are correct, compact, efficient, maintainable, and cheap. Therefore, if someone is missing a few limbs, or a sense or two, they're really not noticeably different from the rest of us in programming ability. The handicapped may need a special piece of apparatus, which is probably not very expensive, but we all decorate our offices with special magical tokens that we feel help our performance. The crafty manager who understands motivation will regard these little investments for the handicapped as money well spent, for handicapped programmers always outperform those programmers who are supposed to have full command of their faculties.

Some managers, though, worry about the effect a handicapped person will have on other workers in the office. According to everything I've heard or observed, the major effect is to make people realize how little they're doing with what they've been given. True, that realization often leads to changes in the organization of programming work, but a manager who can't handle that kind of change ought not to be managing.

When it comes to programming, we're all handicapped, though we may not know it. Because we ordinarily use such a minuscule part of our limited potential, we often outperform ourselves when we have something to prove to the world. Therefore, it's an *advantage* to have a recognized and accepted handicap. If we could only get our universal *mental* handicap recognized and accepted, perhaps programming could become an Olympic event.

What Are the Paradigms
for a Professional Programmer?

The 1978 ACM Turing Award was presented to Robert W. Floyd of Stanford University. His acceptance speech, entitled "The Paradigms of Programming," was published in the August 1979 issue of *Communications of the ACM*. I encourage every reader—everyone connected with programming—to read Floyd's speech. I would also like to advance some of his ideas in another direction.

A paradigm is a pattern—in this case a pattern of thought. Floyd elaborates on a number of paradigms, including

> Structured programming
> Dynamic programming
> Recursive coroutines
> Rule-based systems
> Nondeterministic systems
> Programming languages

He speaks of the mess that is "the state of the art in computer programming" and says,

> Our best hope is to improve our own capabilities. I believe the best chance we have

to improve the general practice of programming is to attend to our paradigms.

Floyd himself has done as much as any other computer person to invent new paradigms, refine existing paradigms, and communicate paradigms clearly to succeeding generations of programmers. I believe he richly deserves the Turing Award for this work. I'm especially pleased that he's taken the occasion of the award to reveal something of the inner workings of his mind—the meta-paradigms, if you will, that have created such a bountiful intellectual outpouring.

The meta-paradigms I've extracted from the essay include the following:

1. Use of analogy, as in relating computer processes to processes in human organizations.
2. Tracing and retracing his own thought processes in solving difficult problems, rather than merely resting content with the solution itself.
3. Induction from specific cases to general rules, and testing these general rules on other specific cases.
4. Reading other people's programs.
5. Deliberately widening his circle of intellectual associates to include those who adhere to "alien conventions," so that reading programs becomes a more fruitful occupation.
6. Attempting to communicate with (teach) others about paradigms, as a way of clarifying his own thought.
7. Actively seeking to know what others have done before, rather then reinventing everything.
8. Using what others have done as a starting point for the question "How could I have invented this?"

As Floyd himself summarizes:

My message to the serious programmer is: spend a part of your working day examining and refining your own methods. Even though programmers are always struggling to meet some future or past deadline, methodological abstraction is a wise long term investment.

If you are a serious programmer, you should heed that advice. You may even want to extend the implicit definition of *paradigm* or *methodological abstraction*. Essentially, all Floyd's examples concern what a programmer does from the time he or she receives a well-defined problem. It is essential to know what to do with well-defined problems, but it's not enough. Why not? Because the working professional programmer spends much more time on ill-defined problems, as when

1. There is a user who doesn't know what the problem is.
2. There is a user who knows what the problem is, but the problem is really something else.
3. There is a user who knows what the problem is, but the programmer doesn't understand, or believe, or listen to the user.
4. There is more than one user, and each is in one or more of the above three situations.
5. The user population changes with time.
6. The problem changes with time.
7. Everyone is screaming and losing presence of mind.

In ill-defined situations, computer programmers tend to take over the definition job and define a problem they'd *like* to solve. Floyd quotes a graffito from a Stanford University graduate student office: "I would rather write programs to help me write programs than write programs." Here we see the healthful activity or methodological abstraction bordering on a disease—a way of avoiding problems on which we don't want to work.

The professional programmer's methodological vocabulary is rich in such problem-avoidance paradigms. We foist them on any unwary customer with the gall to enter our sacred programming office with an ill-defined or uninteresting problem. Someday soon I'm sure to hear a programmer say, "We'll have that program as soon as we work out the proper paradigm, as Professor Floyd taught us to do. In the meantime, don't bother us with *your* problems."

In my opinion—and I doubt that Floyd would disagree—the paradigms for solving well-defined problems are only part of the programmer's responsibility. At least as important are the deeper, fuzzier paradigms about the nature of programming work itself.

For me, the most global of all paradigms is that the professional programmer is *a person who solves problems for other people— whatever that takes.*

Some of the methods that the professional programmer should be working on are these:

1. What should I do about a program for a well-defined problem that I don't believe should be solved at all?
2. How do I determine whether a computer should be used at all?
3. How do I design the overall environment of people and machines in which the computer programs will have to operate?
4. How do I design the computer programs so that they don't have unintended effects on the overall environment in which they operate?
5. How do I work effectively with people whose problems are not well defined, who don't understand as much about computers as I do, who understand more about many other things than I do, and whose motivations are different from mine?
6. How do I change situations in which I cannot work effectively as a professional programmer?
7. How do I create programs that will continue to be good solutions in a future full of uncertainty—a future in which problems change, people change, and in which I won't be around?
8. How do I determine which methodological level is the best to be working on at any particular moment?
9. How do I work on those aspects of my own personality and problem-solving approach that are so personal I can't even see them, even though they may be the most important factor in my effectiveness as a programmer?

Perhaps, though, these are not the concerns of the "computer scientist," who would "rather write programs to help write programs." If not, then whose concerns are they? There seems to be no great army rushing to work on *these* problems—all the more reason why the serious programmer should be working on them personally, as a wise long-term investment.

Can a Professional Be Happy in This Job?

I frequently meet a programmer or analyst who is deeply troubled by the implications of the work of a data processing professional. What we do today with computers may affect the lives of thousands or millions of people for many years to come. Moreover, most of those people won't have any way to relate a discomfort in their lives to what we are doing today. They may sheepishly accept the explanation "That's the way the computer must do it" or the even more insidious "That's the way things are."

Some professionals I know, particularly programmers working in shops where nobody inspects anyone else's work, salve their conscience by sabotaging their employer's information systems. In many cases it's difficult to tell whether this is intentional or unintentional. But in some cases there is no doubt.

Many programmers and analysts have complained to me that their work holds no meaning for them. They don't know what is being done with the piece of program or specification they write, or they do know and don't approve. Their response is to stay on the job, draw the salary, and bad-mouth their employer at every safe opportunity.

I think it's time we stood up to be counted. We have an enormous responsibility to the people whose lives will be affected by our systems. If we don't believe in what our employer is doing, or we don't understand it, then why are we working there? Is it just to draw a fat salary? If so, what does that make us?

For some years, I published a list of principles for programmers and analysts who are seeking a new job. Many people have responded to these principles, saying they were helpful not only in seeking a job, but in considering whether to leave a present job or in trying to change some conditions of employment.

The number of people with these problems seems to be on the increase. To help these people I've revised the principles into the following set of questions that can be used in evaluating a new job or an old job.

1. Are the goals of this organization consonant with my own personal beliefs?
2. Are the goals of my part of the organization clear? Do I agree with them?
3. Does management provide adequate time and resources for my professional development? Is this just by chance, or is there an explicit, continuing commitment to provide both time and resources?
4. Am I evaluated by being pitted against my co-workers? Am I encouraged to cooperate totally to help others achieve their full potential, and are others expected to do so toward me?
5. Do I really understand what I am supposed to be doing? Do I understand why I'm supposed to be doing it? Is this kind of understanding encouraged in the organization?
6. Is my work and the work of others open and available for critical comments by peers? Am I expected to participate in giving and receiving such critical service?
7. Am I really able to devote myself to this organization and this project to the extent that's expected of me?

People who ask these questions and consider the answers seriously don't wind up in jobs that make them miserable.

Asking the questions is not always easy. Sometimes you get an answer you don't like, and you are forced to make a decision. That's not necessarily bad, but it can be hard. One of my colleagues decided he didn't believe in the goals of his project but had taken the job because of the high pay. He left for a lower-paying job, and his family, though a bit poorer, was ecstatic with the happiness it brought them.

Several times, people have reported that their managers were enraged by one of these questions, and they realized that the rage was a sure sign of future trouble. One way or another, they found themselves new managers.

When I published some of these questions in a column, I received many thoughtful replies. Particularly striking was a letter from Jo Edkins. I'd like to share the letter with others and to comment on it part by part, as it unfolds.

After some flattery, to butter the pill, Jo begins:

> I agree completely with the attitude, but being rather cynical, I cannot see the details being practical. The idea of finding out the goals of an organization or project is fine, for organizations of 20 people or less. I belong to a multi-national company, and I doubt if anyone knows its goals.

I agree there are cases in which it is difficult or impossible to know an organization's goals, but let's begin where we do know the goals. I've had several deep discussions with employees of tobacco companies. They may not know the true goals of their organizations, but they have a fair idea of what the companies are doing in the world and it makes them uncomfortable. Under the circumstances, there's really nothing they can do *within* the organization to ease their minds. Of course, not everyone working for these companies feels this way. Many people think tobacco is a great blessing to the human race—my wife happens to be one of them. The question is not whose values are correct, but whether you can work in a situation where good work on your part will perpetuate values you don't believe in. If you leave, you'll be making the greatest possible contribution to your *own* well-being, and you just might help propagate your values. Eventually, if nobody is willing to work for a tobacco company, the companies will be forced out of business by the high cost of obtaining labor.

In many cases where the goals are not clear, perhaps the

answer is that then it doesn't matter. But if it does matter to you that you know what value system you're participating in, your best solution may be to join a company with "20 people or less." That's what I did, and so have many programmers I know, for precisely that reason.

If enough people leave large organizations that are so cumbersome they don't know their own goals, this will add a cost penalty to bigness and to fuzziness. In the end, it could shape our society. It's not much, but it's probably better than working for an organization in which you suspect that the better you perform, the worse the world will be.

But then, not all large companies are quite that fuzzy or have such terrible goals. Which brings me to Jo's next objection:

> Even on a lower level, a rule of management goes "state of knowledge is inversely proportional to desire of imparting same, especially to inferiors." This is just a fact of life. We could all set up our own software companies, but, oh dear!, will the companies that hire us have good goals—and will they tell us about them?

I agree absolutely. Friends of mine brag about their own purity of goals but have contracts with organizations that manufacture poison gas or terrorize nice old ladies who don't understand their gas bills and therefore pay late.

If you are in the software business, or even in the training business, you still have to consider the consequences of your actions. And if you stretch your consideration far enough, you may find something you don't like. I've refused many contracts on that basis, but I do accept people from the CIA and similar organizations in my courses, even though I won't consult with them. My rationalization is that my client in a course is the *person*, not the organization.

And, indeed, a certain number of my students leave the organization that paid their tuition immediately upon completing a course. Interestingly, although I always offer to return the tuition in such cases, every company so far has recognized that it was better off without the dissatisfied employee on the payroll—no matter how good the employee was as a technical person. (As a not altogether irrelevant aside, it bothers me to hear people say that they "belong" to a company or to hear "superior-inferior" terminology used to describe the relationship between two workers. I believe that such terminology eventually influences our thinking, and we actually begin to believe we (or others) *are* inferior, and that we (or they) are, more or less, slaves.)

Jo goes on to tackle one of my own favorite targets, the universities:

> We could become academics, but is the computer that we are maintaining being used for keeping political files on its students, and giving the information to companies? (Damn fool use for a computer anyway.) I prefer to work within the environment I find myself.

Again, I agree completely. Academics are particularly liable to dangerous self-delusion about what their employers are doing. I left a tenured chair in an American university precisely because the university was doing such things as Jo suggests with its computer—and worse. Computer people are in a particularly good position to spot discrepancies between the stated goals of their employers and the employers' actual goals or practices. But *not* if you really don't believe in the public goals in the first place. As Gandhi once said, "If you don't believe in barrooms, then there's no sense getting involved in arguments about segregation in barrooms."

Once you have established this basic agreement with the goals of your organization, then what Jo proposes makes perfect sense:

> The threat of leaving, even with a shortage of programming, is a very blunt instrument, which may miss its mark altogether.

I think I was guilty in my original article of not, as Richard Nixon said, making myself "perfectly clear." I'm quite definitely not proposing that anyone *threaten* to leave their job. If you find the position unacceptable, then either work to make it acceptable or simply leave. Don't threaten. A threat not only may miss its mark, it's almost *guaranteed* to miss its mark. At best your employer will believe you're just trying to get more money, and in any case you'll learn that to large organizations, *nobody* is indispensable.

Can a Professional Be Happy in This Job?   21

If you leave a place, you leave it worse than before (since an active critic has left). If you stay, and complain, and shout, and criticize, and suggest, and persuade, you will find out things, you will make others aware of what is going on, and, just possibly, you might improve the set-up slightly.

I can't improve on that plea, but I can point out that the path Jo proposes can be mighty difficult and lonely. And, if you ultimately fail to have even a slight influence, you may very well crack up and never be able to muster the effort again. For that reason, it is absolutely essential that you first determine whether you can live comfortably within your organization's value system. You do not want to be in the position of attempting to make improvements only to suddenly discover that you have been contributing to something—like poison gas or secret dossiers—that you would rather have destroyed.

It's also essential that there is at least a possibility that your slight improvement has a chance of influencing the overall plan of things. No matter how wonderful that plan is, to work after hope of success has died will only kill that spark within you—the spark you will need to ignite yourself for the next battle.

One of the principal reasons I wrote down that list of questions is that over the past two decades I've seen many good men and women destroy themselves working in futile causes—causes that they really knew were futile from the beginning. After all these years, I've never learned to shrug those people off. Each story hurts as much as the first.

All of these crusaders started out expressing the kind of sentiment that Jo expresses, about their job and the programming profession generally:

The two main fears about computing now are "Privacy" and possible unemployment. I am sometimes afraid of just plain bad programming or system design. What DLVC at Swansea has done to the cause of technological advancement in this country, I hate to think. But it wouldn't have been better if all the best people had left. Good grief! It's only in the last couple of years that the "revolutionary concept" of designing a program before you write it has begun to creep slowly into commercial programming. It was done by people trying to improve things from within.

I've seen my share of computing disasters and I do believe that in most of them, things would have improved if all the best people had left—the earlier the better. I have seen many ill-conceived projects on which the best people have left and have thereby caused the project to collapse before it affected the general public. I know that when all else fails from within an organization, it can be the best thing for the world if you "vote with your feet."

Look at it this way. The managers of the doomed project probably know nothing about the technical state of affairs and can know only through the advice of their "inferiors." One of these inferiors tells them that the company is absolutely committed to a disaster path, but when the managers do nothing, the inferior keeps on working and drawing pay. In such a situation, how can the managers believe what this "inferior" person is trying to tell them? Would you?

Again, I agree with Jo in saying:

> I think the best way to protect the public against bad computing is to educate the public so that it does not accept bad computing. We too can do our piece in our own small sphere of influence, but ultimately safeguards concerning a profession must come from outside that profession. . . . This does not absolve the analyst or programmer from his responsibility. He must do the best he can, but he, alone, cannot possibly tackle the entire problem.

In the end, there's no way we can "educate the public so that it does not accept bad computing" if we ourselves accept bad computing. We must learn to recognize situations that will almost inevitably produce bad computing *before* we allow ourselves to become entangled in them, financially and emotionally.

Naturally, nobody can predict the future with certainty. The best we can do is look to our past and try to extract some general principles that would have kept us out of trouble had we applied them earlier. We must make our share of mistakes, but life is too short to learn everything by bitter experience. And there are plenty of truly worthwhile things to do with computers, so we need not fear leaving some stupid, miserable, or downright nasty job undone. What better way to get the public to respect our profession rather than fear and mock it, as so many people do now? As Jo says:

> I do agree with you that DP people should look beyond their pay packets and promotion prospects to the responsibilities of their jobs. Good luck in your attempts to make them do so!

> Good luck in *your* attempts!

The Impatient Psychiatrist:
A Fable

A psychiatrist had been having trouble with his patients all day, but George was particularly uncooperative. The psychiatrist was beginning to doubt his professional competence and searched his memory for tried-and-true tricks of the trade that might be used on the recalcitrant George.

He decided to attempt free association. "George," he explained, "I want you to clear your mind of all thoughts. Make it completely blank. Then when I tap my pencil, I want you to tell me the first thing that comes into your mind."

At the signal, George said, "I want you to kiss me, doctor."

The psychiatrist was furious but, as this was not a proper professional pose, subdued the anger. "That's not satisfactory, George," came the reply. "You're repeating an old pattern, which we know you should be trying to erase. I want you to try again. Just clear that thought out of your mind and then tell me what you're thinking."

George tried, but then said in a pitiful tone, "I'm sorry, doctor. No matter how hard I try, all I can think of is that I want you to kiss me."

Now the doctor's anger began to creep into the response. "That won't do, George. Just think of something else."

"I can't think of anything else. I just want you to kiss me."

Losing all control, the psychiatrist screamed, "If I've told you once, I've told you a thousand times, I'm not going to kiss you. So get that thought out of your mind."

"But why won't you kiss me?" pleaded George.

"Why won't I kiss you? Why, I shouldn't even be here on the couch with you!"

MORAL: Once you're on the couch together, it's too late to worry about the kissing.

ALTERNATIVELY: When you find yourself perpetually angered by little questions in your professional life, perhaps the problem is some bigger question you answered wrong earlier.

Part II

How Do Professionals Get That Way?

Programmers Are Too Valuable to Be Trusted to Computers

Choosing a Teaching Language

Every four years, along with county elections, the local computer science professors raise the question of the correct teaching language for programming. There's a lot of brave talk about throwing the rascals out, many lunches devoted to campaigning, a wave of confidence just before the election, and then the ultimate defeat of the upstart. In the end, both FORTRAN and the sheriff are reelected. They may be corrupt; they may be incompetent; they may be creaking with age; but at least they're familiar.

Like the county voters, professors are quite ready to rationalize the result. As the years since 1956 have accumulated, the points in these arguments have, one by one, withered away. And yet one remains, year after year, the backbone of conservatism everywhere. To quote a genuine professor:

> My decision to base this course on the WATFIV programming language was founded not only on a recognition of real-world applications but also on the raw economics of computer costs at our installation.

Real-world and *raw economics* are no-nonsense words—none of your ivory-tower folderol. Let's look, therefore, at some of the raw economics of computer costs for training in the real world.

Twenty years ago, computers were *really* expensive—so expensive that FORTRAN had to be ruled out of consideration for the language used in a programming course. In fact, even the richest of the rich thought using a computer in a programming course was a frivolous extravagance.

Twenty years is a long time in a sheriff's life, and even longer in the life of the programming profession. Few remember those days, or even believe that it was possible to teach programming without a computer. Soon, at the rate personal computers are spreading, few will remember what it was like to learn computing with a *teacher*. In the few years since that WATFIV decision was rationalized, the raw economics have changed so sharply that we could almost afford to give each student a personal computer. In this modern age, it sounds archaic to say "our installation" in the singular. What university worth accreditation hasn't got a dozen or more minis and micros scattered around the campus like homecoming handbills?

Still, the FORTRAN argument has survived the latest reduction in hardware costs. Now it is the micros that can't afford to run anything else—except, heaven forbid, BASIC. Where does this conservatism originate? Where will it end? How far will it spread? Why does it resist the repeated efforts of language designers and implementers to break it down?

Using Software Tools

The programming language is merely the oldest and most familiar software tool, and universities are merely the oldest and most familiar tools for social change. The same conservatism in the adoption of new tools is found for all other tools in all other institutions. If we can answer our questions, the payoff could be staggering.

Of the many reasons for nonuse of new tools, perhaps the most obvious is the lack of attention given to training. An elephantine sum of money has been spent on the development of software tools—the current rate probably exceeds a billion dollars a year. In contrast, a microorganismic sum of money has been spent on training people to use those tools.

Most of the tools—perhaps as a consequence of this disparity between development and training—are never, or hardly ever, used. Not only do people continue to use FORTRAN, but they continue to use it without, for instance, even getting cross-reference listings of their program variables. Even when their FORTRAN compiler provides such a cross-reference, the installation disables it, usually as a "standard," because "it costs too much." Even where it is routinely produced, 90 percent of the programmers never look at it; yet the cross-reference listing is one of the simplest software tools—one of the most direct in its use, one of the most convenient, and one of the most ancient.

The situation is little better in the majority of installations that have abandoned FORTRAN for "higher" languages. As an exercise in formal review techniques, our clients and students study published programs, which presumably are held up as examples for novices to follow. In a typical review of a program written by two professors of computer science, we studied the use of PL/I. Although the specifications offered ideal situations for employing each of them, none of the following PL/I facilities were used:

1. Dynamic allocation of storage
2. Cross-section notation
3. Array expressions
4. Factoring of attributes
5. Subscript expressions
6. Control of type conversions
7. Bit strings

One could almost have removed the semicolons and, in effect, compiled the program on a FORTRAN compiler.

As is typical, further examination of the program revealed no impact of the years of discussion on programming style. The following are among the more pitiful stylistic practices we found:

1. Intricate branching, including into and out of loops
2. Superfluous statements based on incomplete understanding of the action of earlier statements

Programmers Are Too Valuable to Be Trusted to Computers   31

3. Initialization of variables upon exit from loops that used them
4. Use of single-character names such as K and R
5. Use and reuse of scalar variables in a program not pressed for storage
6. Use of a name with two different meanings, one in the program and one in a comment explaining its meaning
7. Use of the keyword PTR as a data name in a most confusing context
8. General inconsistency in the naming of variables
9. Computations inefficiently placed within loops, yet rendered inaccessible to an optimizer, in a program that heavily used pointers "for efficiency"

At the level of design, the program again showed no influence of recent discussion in the industry, let alone design tools and concepts. We found

1. No checking whatsoever for valid input—either bounds or values
2. Unchecked input used to control calculations, as in computed branches
3. A completely undesigned and error-prone input format
4. An algorithm that was inefficient for all but small cases of input
5. No monitoring of performance of the algorithm, which might have indicated loss of performance to the user
6. Incomprehensible error messages
7. Comprehensible error messages that were wrong or misleading

In our work, we have reviewed hundreds of programs from dozens of installations. The programs display approximately the same range of problems, and the installations display approximately the same nonuse of tools. At least 75 percent of the installations routinely debug using unformatted hexadecimal dumps. At least 90 percent have never used a preprocessor. Program libraries are coming into use, but are still not found in more than 50 percent of installations. Test data generation is rare; archiving of test data is even more rare; and even a rudimentary data-set comparison is hardly ever used.

We're not speaking of the number of these tools that sit on the shelf, accumulating dust and rent. We are counting the tool as used if anyone uses it, even if for a minor part of its capabilities. Consequently, these figures overestimate real professional use. Since we are spending money on training, what can it possibly be teaching programmers?

The Computer as Instructor

In view of the inadequate use of our expensive tools, it is obvious that we are not teaching programmers to use the computer adequately in their programming work. The conclusion seems obvious—we must spend more on computers in our classes, not less.

Obvious? It would seem so, until we look at the way the computer is being used in classes. Indeed, we are not teaching the students at all—the computer is carrying the burden for us. As a result, we find ourselves standing on both sides of the same fence. It is the double thesis of this section that (1) the computer is insufficiently used in programmer education, and (2) the computer is overused in programmer education.

Let's examine how the computer is used in a typical university course in programming. The nature of this use may best be understood in terms of an analogy. Suppose we have succeeded in developing a "paper-grader" program for high school English courses and that we have succeeded in getting the program used within the high schools in the following way:

1. The teacher lectures on one topic or another to 50 to 500 students.
2. The teacher gives an assignment to write an essay.
3. The students write an essay, under strict orders not to help anyone else or to receive help from anyone else.
4. The essay is graded by our computer program on the basis of spelling errors and grammatical errors.
5. The paper is returned to the students with a grade.

What do you suppose the students will learn?

The reason this analogy works is that we don't have to guess what the students will learn. We already know. Even without the computer, this is the way many high school English teachers conduct their classes in composition, and the results are notoriously bad. Many of the students learn to spell; some learn to avoid incorrect grammar; essentially none learn to communicate. (Fortunately, a few learn these things from other experiences.)

In programming education, the "paper grader" is already built into the compiler. Because programming assignments must be recycled through the grader until all "spelling and grammar" errors are eliminated, the emphasis on these aspects is all the stronger. In many classes the professor has no time or stomach for reading the actual programs. Sometimes not even the outputs are read. In such classes, students turning in wrong outputs never find this out from the instructor. Students turning in fake outputs are never found out *by* the instructor.

To solve the problem of unread output, sophisticated schools have developed "grader" programs that exercise the student programs using test inputs and scoring the resultant outputs. Graders definitely raise the level of computer assistance—but mostly to the harried instructor, not to the student. After all, for classes with hundreds of neophytes, how else can the legions of warm bodies be handled economically, or handled at all?

To give them their due, grader programs actually can represent an advance over the simple compiler checking that most schools still use. But, again, what is it they teach? By reviewing programs produced by these students, in class and years later, you can learn what the computer teaches about programming:

1. Accurate card punching, in a batch environment
2. Use of a text editor to overcome inaccurate keying, in an on-line environment
3. Spelling of keywords
4. Consistent spelling of programmer-chosen words
5. A subset of the syntax of a programming language

But beyond these important lessons, the computer—used in these ways—teaches a much deeper lesson, one that will remain long after the WATFIV syntax is forgotten. That lesson is

Programs are shown to be correct by testing them.

This is a curious lesson. To quote the original sermon on structured programming by Edsger Dijkstra:

> The extent to which the program correctness can be established is not purely a function of the program's external specifications and behaviour but depends critically on its internal structure.

In short, what the computer is teaching is precisely antithetical to the principal lesson of the strongest movement for improved programming since the invention of the assembler. It is teaching this lesson every day, in every school in the country, to thousands and thousands of present and potential programmers.

But there is a second high-level lesson—a meta-lesson, actually—a lesson about learning itself:

> We learn to program by throwing garbage into a computer and seeing what comes out.

This lesson is like the prejudices of our youth—deeply set and hard to change. What's more, it's being taught earlier and deeper, now that personal computers are so readily available. What are we going to do with the next generation of programmers?

Render unto the Computer . . .

Computers are excellent at teaching—about computers. No amount of lecturing about syntax errors seems to make the slightest impression on the majority of students—unless it is a slightly negative one. A compiler, though, patiently and mercilessly teaches syntax to one recalcitrant student after another. Cleverly used, the compiler as teacher can even motivate some students to learn principles of syntax, though they have to obtain those principles elsewhere.

Some toolmakers say that syntax and spelling are unimportant lessons because tools can be built to correct any errors. I can agree with them only partly, for no system will ever be able to correct *all* errors of any type. Consequently, even the most brilliant programmer must at some time learn the hard lessons of syntax and spelling—or else waste hundreds of frustrating hours.

Furthermore, even when the most sophisticated and careful proof techniques are applied to the most magnificently structured program, the computer may reveal two kinds of error that can slip through. First, there are the simple proofreading errors—errors that plague the most advanced mathematics journals as well as the most humble programs. Second, there is the complete misunderstanding of the problem.

Though a programmer may prove that the program does what she thinks it does, she can never prove that what she thinks it should do is what the user or users want it to do. In one sense, there are no wrong programs, only *different* programs. The only hope we have of discovering if we've solved the right problem is to give the proposed solution back to the originator.

Consider the following typical example. A professor of archaeology was teaching a large introductory course, assisted by a computer that printed individualized examinations drawn at random from a pool of questions. An advanced student in the computer science department had been given the job of writing the program to print the exams, but the program had one slight flaw. Rather frequently, one exam would contain the same question twice, or even three times. Rather than sampling the question pool "without replacement," the program was sampling "with replacement."

The professor noticed this defect and confronted the student. He was told that the program could sample without replacement, but that the process was "very inefficient." He knew that the professor certainly would not want to pay the extra cost, so it would be better to print, say, fourteen questions to be sure of getting ten unique ones. The students just had to be told to answer "the first ten unique questions."

The reader may want to speculate just which of the many poor algorithms this student programmer had chosen. In fact, the technique was conceptually very simple. When sampling without replacement was specified, the program would produce a tentative exam and then test to see if it contained any repeated questions. During program test, ten questions were being drawn from a pool of twenty, which meant that about thirty exams had to be drawn to get one without duplicates!

We must be careful to draw the correct moral from this tale. Most professors of computer science would lament this student's miserable ignorance of algorithms. Although this kind of ignorance is sad, we could learn to live with it in the "real world." What we can't live with is this student's ignorance of the programmer's role in life.

It was not the programmer's place to decide how much the professor wanted to spend on exams. His guess about what the professor wanted led him to authorize printing of several thousand exams that had to be discarded. The deadline was missed, and the old system of a typed exam had to be used. Unless one is programming for one's own amusement, the final decision about whether a program is correct rests not with the computer, not with the programmer, but with the party with the problem.

Another relevant point, of course, is that the programmer had not the slightest idea that his program was wrong. He didn't even know it was wrong from an efficiency point of view. Neither the computer nor the professor could teach that lesson.

There are, in the end, a multitude of lessons one must learn to become a truly professional programmer. Each such lesson has its own characteristic ways of being learned. In designing programming courses, we must see that each lesson is taught in the most effective way and not merely that a certain number of students can be "processed" for a whole semester without demanding a tuition refund.

How to Teach a Programming Course With or Without a Computer

How do we design such an effective programming course? The general pattern should now be clear:

1. Use the computer to teach what only the computer can teach.
2. Use people to teach what only people can teach.
3. Make the economic choice between computer and people only in those cases where either can do the job with equal effectiveness.

No doubt an introductory course ought to begin with one or two encounters with the machine to teach:

1. The overall process by which programs get created
2. The finicky nature of computing machines
3. The mismatch between such machines and our abilities to be precise

After these lessons are taught, at least on an introductory level, the class should turn to its human resources to learn more difficult lessons. A typical assignment might involve

1. A problem posed by the instructor acting as "user" but with certain lessons in mind
2. Each student making a trial solution, on paper
3. Each student evaluating the trial solution of another student
4. Small groups of students, sometimes with instructor supervision, arriving at a composite solution
5. Trying the composite on the machine
6. Groups exchanging solutions for more formal review, sometimes guided by the instructor in front of the entire class

In such a class, the students ingest a much richer and more meaningful diet of programming information. They avoid time wasted on syntax and spelling, which are corrected as a by-product of the formal evaluations and which can be taught by machine— except that it's actually cheaper and more effective to do it through reviews. From teacher to student, and from student to student, passes knowledge about style, language, algorithms, design, tools, and hundreds of little pieces of programming wisdom that collectively set apart the professional from the amateur. And were it not too presumptuous, we might have mentioned that once in a while knowledge even passes from student to teacher.

But what of the "raw economics"? We've speculated about this. We've experimented with it. Our experiments surpass even our wildest speculations. Of course, the first saving comes because teams of five students run only one-fifth the number of assignments through the computer. Yet the lessons for each student are far greater than the old secretive method, for each student sees many approaches, not just one.

Second, the number of runs to produce a correct program (and not just a "working" program) is drastically reduced. The magnitude of reduction depends somewhat on the size of the problem, but a typical figure for student batch problems is from an average of twenty runs to an average of two runs. Actually, most programs run correctly the first time on the machine—and the students can demonstrate it. They had better be able to—if not, the other teams cut it to pieces.

Third, the programs themselves typically will run more efficiently once attention is focused on design rather than on grammar and spelling. The factor of 30 lost by the archaeologist's programmer would not be untypical, but suppose we modestly take this factor as 2. Putting the three factors together we reduce machine costs by a factor of about 100 ($5 \times 10 \times 2$). Certainly that's enough raw economics to permit us to choose our programming tools on the basis of what they will teach, not what they will cost.

But the benefits to education do not stop with machine economics. We can use this method quite successfully when there is no compiler for the language we want to teach, when there is no compiler at all, and even when there is no class. When the probability that a program will work the first time is so high, in many circumstances there is not much to be gained from actually running the program. Getting rid of the computer, or at the very least controlling the incredible variance it usually introduces, permits us to plan with more confidence and to stick with the plan as the semester unfolds. Indeed, once freed of the constraints of the machine, the course economics depend mostly on the availability of teacher and classroom. Once beyond the barest introduction, any group of programmers can teach themselves in this way, on the job or off.

Actually, the economics of on-the-job training reverses the usual college assumptions. The students are likely to be making higher salaries than the instructor, and they certainly are when considered as a class. It simply doesn't pay to transport professional programmers to a crosstown campus for programming lectures when they can learn much more in less time by inspecting each other's work.

There is an implicit challenge here to the professional teacher who wants to stay out of the unemployment lines. With the right leader, a small group of programmers can multiply their learning through review techniques. The leader has to help them invest the money saved on lectures and machine time in fruitful alternatives, such as instrumented runs that permit them to make design and algorithm comparisons that would be difficult to perform analytically.

The leader can give them more problems to do in the same time or guide them in exploring more alternatives to the same problems. In this way, the students can be nudged along the path to design rather than to even more obscure bit-twiddling. Tools can be evaluated in actual use, perhaps giving some return for the billions we've invested in them. But it will take a lot of running for an instructor to stay ahead in such an environment.

This new environment may not suit the old-fashioned teacher who sees the instructor job as a kind of Olivier playing Hamlet to packed houses of sleeping students. And it may not suit the typical computer jockey whose narrow mind and dogged persistence have served to get so many A's from the usual programming classes. If such people are thus encouraged to leave the programming profession, it can be counted as another plus for this system of professional education.

Some Future History

If we study the development of other high-technology fields such as electrical engineering, machine tools, telephonics, steam power, and printing, we see that computing is not unique. We may be going through the stages faster, but we're going through them all the same. Our first quarter century has been fast-paced and driven almost entirely by the technological imperative. Hardware sales have been the alpha and omega of our narrow world. Anything that didn't promote the sale of more hardware was left behind in the rush for survival in the technology jungle.

For the past few years, since IBM "unbundled," the sales managers have come to understand that software is a product, just like hardware—but with an even greater potential market. The software rush is now in its adolescent stage, and it is repeating the entire hardware history at an even faster pace.

Yet today, after an investment of perhaps 200 billion dollars in hardware and software, the achievements are relatively small. Relative to what? If history is any guide, relative to what the future holds in store. One measure of our immaturity is the lack of any true programming profession. The career path of choice for programmers today is "up and out." Most programmers have nothing to learn after mastery of grammar and spelling, so there is little economic incentive for companies to retain a higher-paid "experienced" programmer when a freshly trained beginner is available at a beginner's salary.

And when an individual does surpass this narrow training, there is nobody in management to recognize how valuable such a professional really is. The managers, after all, once took a "programming" course. They know that programming is unprofessional, shallow, and unmanageable. They know that money spent on training is wasted and would be better invested in some new hardware or a software tool that promises to replace a few programmers.

All of us have been hypnotized by a running sales pitch consisting of fallacious "raw economics" and illusory "real worlds." We have spent billions for tools, but not pennies on understanding what is needed to create the professional technical leaders who will actually use them. We've spent millions on "schooling" but have skimped on real learning. As a result, our tools lie on the shelf, misunderstood and little used. Our systems seem to cost too much, but conference after conference merely repeats the sales pitch of its predecessor—buy more *things*! Our systems fail to satisfy, but all we hear is that people don't understand the finicky nature of computers—the *next* generation will solve all that!

The next generation will come when we outgrow our adolescent fascination with toys and develop an adult interest in people. Then we will begin, as other technologies have done, to master the social and psychological forces that are the real power behind successful technology—and the real reason for technology in the first place. An excellent starting point would be to take computer training out of the hands of computers, and perhaps put it in the brains of people.

Training for Flexibility

I have another letter from my most stimulating correspondent, Jo Edkins, that poses the following problem of interest to many of us today:

> Training is quite a substantial part of my job, and I am training some graduates to be COBOL programmers at the moment. . . . Schools and universities are being flooded with computers of all shapes, sizes, makes, and reliability. The main language is BASIC, FORTRAN is second, with PASCAL and ALGOL in hot pursuit. Out of sixteen graduates only two had never written a computer program. Compare this with a few years ago! Yet only three had written COBOL and none had written PL/I. This education is supposed to "fit them for the world of computers" and yet they found their knowledge a handicap, a drawback, or a confusion. The ones with no computer experience seemed to accept concepts as they came, while the others were trying to fit them in with concepts they already knew. Of course, we tried to help them reconcile their differing knowledge,

but you try coping with BASIC, FORTRAN, ALGOL, PAS-
CAL, APL, etc., simultaneously! I don't even know the last
two!

What was more worrying was that quite a few of them
found the concepts of data and file hard to understand. Many
people complain that the computer industry tends to want
experienced programmers, and wonder why they can't use some
of these people who have "learnt" about computers! Most firms
just cannot afford the money or time to cope with not only the
necessary learning, but, now, the unlearning that must precede
it. I'm not blaming the graduates themselves (I wouldn't dare
to—they'd have my hide). They have honestly tried their hardest to learn about computers at college, and then had to unlearn
that and learn different concepts.

What do you think about this?

As it happens, I tumbled backward into a solution for this
problem about twenty years ago. Herb Leeds and I had written a
highly successful book, *Computer Programming Fundamentals,* on
assembly-language programming. When it came time for a second
edition, the publisher asked if we couldn't "write something on
FORTRAN," which was the up and coming language of the future.
We were appalled at the prospect of lowering ourselves to teach
any but the "best" language—assembler—but we finally hit upon
a method of keeping our hands free of stain. We taught FORTRAN
in parallel with assembler, showing each example developed in both
languages. I believe that we secretly thought that anybody seeing
both approaches would naturally choose assembler over the infidel,
FORTRAN.

Writing the book taught us many things—lessons I carried
over into my classroom work. Eventually our approach was developed into a full-blown method—one that not only prevents Jo's
problem but has some important extra benefits.

The essence of the method was to teach not a language, but
a *contrasting pair* of languages. Originally it was assembler and
FORTRAN, though many pairs were tried and worked well. Eventually I settled on APL and PL/I for maximum contrast. Most of
the important programming concepts can be illustrated using those
two languages. In situations where APL and PL/I don't illustrate

a concept, they at least give the student a clear understanding that no single language is the "right" way to program.

Each classroom exercise, right from the beginning, was to be done in *both* languages. Along with the two exercises the student had to submit a discussion of why the program turns out differently in the two languages. Quite often in writing these discussions, students "discover" new programming concepts that aren't in either language.

On each exercise, every student reviewed another student's solution. By reviewing, students learned not only languages, but different programming styles as well.

After a classroom presentation of one student's solution, other students were invited to present variations of that solution or entirely different solutions. When looking only at their own work, most people learned slowly, and they learned very little. When looking at the work of others, they learned quickly and deeply.

When we used this "bilingual" method in the university, we avoided the kind of language chauvinism Jo describes. A first language is easy to learn. If you don't believe that, listen to three-year-old Chinese kids chattering up a storm. A third language is easy, too, and the fourth and fourteenth are almost trivial. It's the *second* one that's killing us. When we use the bilingual strategy, there is no second language, so the problem tends to disappear.

Can the bilingual strategy be used in a commercial environment? Yes, if the students are truly novices. But what about those who already know one language? The first step must be to convince the students that what they already know is not sufficient for their new environment.

There are several ways to do this, but the one I prefer is in the form of a challenge. We say that a truly professional programmer should be able to pick up a new programming language and become productive in two weeks of self-study. Our bilingual students were able to do this when they took jobs. If your students are actually able to do this, then they can be excused from the formal class, which solves Jo's problem right there. If they can't—and they may have to try and fail—then they are ready to receive bilingual training.

To use this strategy successfully, the teacher had better be able to demonstrate multilingual proficiency. Indeed, it would be best if the teacher is fluent in *all* the languages the students might know. (That's right, Jo, get yourself a book on APL, and another on PASCAL.) Otherwise the students will try to intimidate you by displaying their "superior" knowledge. Instead of being intimidated, the proficient teacher will harness this prior knowledge and turn it to everyone's advantage. Start by acknowledging that programming is difficult. Explain that programmers need all the help they can get, so that insights from any language will always be valuable to the class. Encourage them to share ways of thinking about the class problems—ways they may have learned from their exposure to other languages. Each time they do this, point out how it illustrates the importance of knowing more than one approach.

At first, some of them will whine about not having some "neat" feature of BASIC that's lacking in COBOL. When this happens, be firm in asserting that although BASIC may give insights into COBOL programming, they are here to learn to be *professionals*. Professionals produce programs in the assigned language, not whining excuses why they can't do the job. When such confrontations arise, I always challenge the student with the ancient observation that "it's a poor worker who blames the tools."

The image the teacher wants to keep uppermost is that of the professional. You're not teaching the students COBOL, you're teaching them to be professional programmers who will, in the immediate future, work in COBOL. If they are already professionals, you won't have this second-language syndrome, and teaching the requisite amount of COBOL should be a snap.

In the light of the transition from amateur to professional, the teacher can see the way to solve many other problems, such as the issue of data and files. The students, in leaving their amateur days behind, are also making the transition from small systems to big systems. This difference shows most easily in data design and files, but it also appears in many other places. For instance, there is the problem of communicability of a program from one person to another. Many of the "school" languages lack just those features needed for constructing large systems. They can't readily handle large amounts of data from many sources. Nor do they succeed when the system must be worked on by many different people.

If you have several students who know one school language,

such as BASIC or PASCAL, you might have them construct a parallel solution to a relatively large case problem. Take a production program and have them translate it into their favorite language. They'll learn many things. Most of all, they'll learn that a professional programmer must be much more flexible than an amateur.

The Cricket Who Wanted to Play Cricket: A Fable

A rather young and impetuous cricket was sitting on his hearth one evening, listening to some people discussing the test matches between England and Australia. He didn't know what England was, let alone Australia, for he usually played hooky from his geography class, but he paid a lot of attention when he heard the word *cricket* being bandied about. He figured out that cricket was a very highly regarded activity, and so he immediately decided that this must be his destiny. He also learned that the great match was to begin the following Thursday at Bournemouth and, although he knew what Thursday was, he didn't have any idea where Bournemouth might be, so he set off immediately to see his geography professor.

The professor was delighted to see a spark of interest in his poorest pupil, but when he found out why the cricket was interested in geography he was disappointed to say the least. "Look here, young fellow," he said, unable to drop the patronizing tone he always adopted with students —a tone that was one of the reasons the cricket could not abide school. "Look here. If you think you are cut out for playing cricket because you

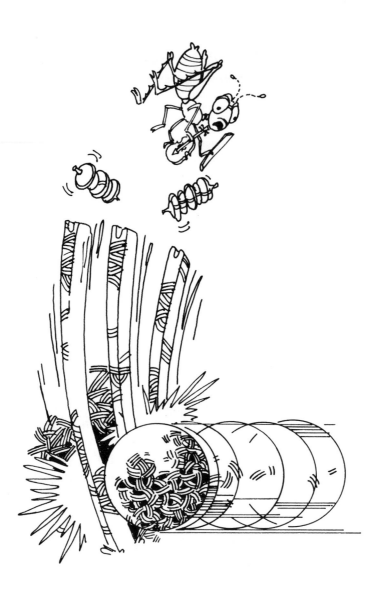

happen to *be* a cricket, you are making a serious error in scholarship. Although the etymology of the name *cricket* is not known for certain, it is probably a corruption of the word *wicket.* Your name, on the other hand, is not a matter of etymology, but one of entomology. Thus, your desire to play cricket is merely the result of a semantic error and would surely disappear if you were better educated. Why not stay here where you are entitled to a free education? That would certainly serve you better and cost less than adventures on the playing fields."

But the cricket had no patience for this kind of scholarship. So after extracting the information he wanted, he set off immediately for the action that was to begin next Thursday (for crickets don't travel very fast). Indeed, by the time he arrived, the match had already begun, and Australia was batting. Rather than take a seat among the spectators, he set out immediately to get himself into the center of the action, which seemed to be close to some wooden stumps set up in the middle of the field. As he was very small, he was able to reach the stumps without disturbing the match, but because of his size he was not able to see what was going on very well. Not knowing anything about cricket—least of all what a wicket was—he decided to climb up on top of the stumps to get a better view. And so he happened to be sitting on top of the wicket when the English bowler stumped the best Australian batsman. As the wicket tumbled off the stumps, carrying the hapless cricket to a hard knock on the ground, an enormous cheer went up from the crowd. The cricket naturally thought the cheer was for him, but he didn't enjoy it for long, as the pain of his broken knee soon rendered him unconscious. When he awoke, it was already dark and the day's play was finished. All through the long, cold, and painful journey home, the cricket thought to himself, "It was certainly a marvelous feeling to have the crowd cheering my brave fall, but I think I will give up cricket, now that I have reached the pinnacle of success."

MORAL: The school of hard knocks has a dear tuition, but some won't learn in any cheaper school.

The Cricket Who Wanted
to Play Baseball: A Fable

While recovering from his cricket injuries, the cricket, not being able to do much else, attended his geography class. There he learned about America, where the national game was not cricket, but a derivative of cricket called baseball. Not being of a scholarly bent, and in spite of his experiences, he soon took a longing for faraway places and, remembering the roar of the crowd much better than the pain in his knee, he set off for America as soon as he was able to jump once again.

"I believe I shall play for the Braves," he thought to himself during the long journey, "for I have certainly demonstrated my bravery on the cricket fields of England. On the other hand, I must be wary of the Cardinals, for everyone knows what Cardinals like to do with crickets." And so, finally, he found himself in Braves Stadium on the afternoon of a big game between the Braves and the Giants.

Still longing to be in the center of the action, he refused to take a seat in the grandstand but went directly toward home plate. "This time," he thought, "I will stay off the stumps, and near to the ground. I may not be able to see so well, but forewarned is forearmed." Thus he betook himself of the flattest seat he could find, which happened to be home plate itself. There he was safe enough until the bottom of the ninth inning when, with the score tied, a runner tried to score from second base on a single. The play was close: the ball, the catcher, and the runner all arrived at home plate in a single cloud of dust and, as the umpire shouted "Safe," an enormous roar arose from the crowd. That roar was still echoing in the cricket's ears many hours later, as he lay on home plate in the empty stadium—this time with both knees broken. "It's a hard life I've chosen," he thought, "but after all is said and done, isn't it worth it, to have such applause?"

MORAL: Experience doesn't necessarily teach anything.

Part III

Why Do Programmers Behave the Way They Do?

Personal Chemistry
and the Healthy Body

Many DP professionals aspire to executive careers yet are mystified each time they are passed over for promotion. Perhaps the problem is in their "personal chemistry."

I have a newspaper clipping quoting J. Gerald Simmons, president of Handy Associates, an executive search firm. (Put aside your prejudice against people who use their first initial and middle name, like J. Edgar Hoover or G. Marvin Weinberg, and hear the man out.) Simmons emphasizes the importance of "personal chemistry" in choosing among otherwise equally qualified candidates. Among the ingredients of personal chemistry are appearance, personality, style, articulateness, energy, attitude, thoughtfulness, composure, sparkle, breadth of interest, and an aura of leadership. These desirable qualities sound a bit like the Boy Scout creed, but let's not give up yet.

Simmons asserts that personal chemistry can be developed, lending hope to the troubled masses yearning to be executives. But his advice on how to develop this chemistry often has the phony ring of a counterfeit coin. For instance:

Appearance: Conspicuous obesity or extreme emaciation are negative marks. (Advice: lose or gain weight.)

Energy, drive, ambition: Cultivate the quick stride, fresh appearance, and tone of superb physical health.

Composure: The nail-biter, hair-twirler, foot-tapper, chain-smoker, or twitcher rarely gets past one interview. (Advice: try to eliminate distracting habits.)

Aura of leadership: An erect carriage, a head held high, an agreeable manner, eye contact, and a certain amount of self-confidence connote leadership qualities.

When I read such items, I'm reminded of my mother nagging me to "sit up straight" or my teacher bellowing "don't chew gum." The advice, when given, seems to me to be less than useless. Worrying about whether you emit an aura of leadership is apt to drive you to nail-biting, mouth-stuffing, or simple mind-squashing.

Yet there's no doubt that Simmons is right. We'd all prefer to be in the presence of people who are nice-looking, energetic but composed, and agreeable. The problem is what to do about it if we're not that way. If you're depressed about life, the easiest thing in the world is to attract advice: "Don't be depressed." Or are you obese? Then how about this advice: "Don't eat so much." Ambrose Bierce defined advice as the smallest current coin. Advice is usually free—and worth every penny. To my mind, most of the advice about "personal chemistry" or other success formulas merely serves to becloud the very few deep principles of true happiness and success. Bertrand Russell wrote about these in his classic book *The Conquest of Happiness,* a book I try to reread every year to restore me to the simple track. I say "try" because my copies are always out on loan and tend not to return. Just now I can't find a copy around the house or office, but Russell's number-one point doesn't need any reminding.

According to Russell, perhaps the greatest philosopher of our century, health comes before all else in producing happiness. Or perhaps it goes the other way—lack of health destroys any other formula that promises success. Consider Simmons's "personal chemistry." If you're healthy, you won't look obese or emaciated. Your stride will naturally be quick. You'll look and smell fresh without spraying your body with a thousand unpronounceable ingredients. You'll probably not bite nails, twirl hair, tap your foot, or drum your fingers. You'll do very little twitching and probably no smoking at all. You'll sit up straight and you probably won't look like you're having trouble digesting your lunch simply because you're not having trouble digesting your lunch.

By curious coincidence, the modern view of health is that it's largely a matter of body chemistry (you are what you eat) and activity (you are what you do). If that's the case, then perhaps "personal chemistry" is no more than "real" chemistry and physics—about as basic as you can get. But rather than give you advice, let me just relate some stories.

We all know Gary Gulper, that dedicated programmer who's dedicated mostly to stuffing his face with junk food. He thinks he's impressing the boss by working through lunch and eating only a candy bar and a Coke from the vending machine. Then there's Susan Sitter—her secret formula for success is to work sixteen hours a day, hoping the boss will notice before she dies for lack of exercise or is immobilized from calluses on the butt.

I'm well acquainted with such people because I display all their qualities. What we share is an honest dedication to our work —so much dedication that we abuse our own bodies, if necessary, to get the work done. Now there's nothing wrong with honest dedication, until it's carried to the point where it destroys our ability to work effectively. What's the sense of working over-over-overtime if in so doing we cause the quality of our work to deteriorate? Why skip lunch for a candy bar to accomplish a task that we'd accomplish much more quickly with a properly nourished brain and relaxed body?

Well, let's be honest with ourselves. It's *fun* to abuse our bodies once in a while. Who can honestly deny the seductiveness of a candy feast, a beverage binge, or an all-night work orgy? So, while we can argue that we're doing it out of dedication to our work, we've got a perfect excuse for fulfilling our innermost desires. And besides, a little excess never hurt anyone, did it? And sometimes the job really does require an all-out, self-sacrificing effort.

Okay, so here comes the moralizing. Too many professionals —including me—develop the habit of sacrificing their bodies to their work. They develop this habit when they are young, when their bodies are much more resilient. Then one day they discover that their bodies don't snap back as quickly or as easily as they once did. But when they discover this deficiency, it's usually far too late, for several reasons:

1. The habit is too ingrained to be gotten rid of easily.
2. The deficiency has been there for a long time before it gets bad enough for them to notice it. But others have been noticing for a long time, so their career has already suffered.
3. They're too old to learn new habits readily.
4. The troubles with their health are likely to multiply, and we all know how hard it is to deal with two interacting system errors.
5. Even if they do start cutting back on excessive workloads and spending time on proper eating and exercise, the results won't be immediately forthcoming—which means that the immediate effect is less output at work and possible loss of job or position.

All that sounds like moralizing. I certainly thought so twenty years ago when people told me such things. Morality, I suppose, is the wisdom that prevents sacrificing long-term happiness for short-term happiness. In the case of health, we need some simple morals because our brain is the first organ to degrade when our health deteriorates. Not only do we feel bad, but we can't apply our brain to the problem because it's in trouble too. But because it's in trouble, it's not likely to see that it's in trouble. When the brain starts to falter, the owner is always the last to know. Morality fails, though, when it congeals into rules whose purpose has long been forgotten. In that sense, morality is just like DP standards. I don't believe people should do things for reasons they don't understand—things like looking healthy, eating spinach, or avoiding GO TO statements. Rules without reasons focus on the appearance of things, not the substance. That's why I'd never dare suggest that people try to improve their personal chemistry by working on the surface.

Instead, I advocate getting underneath. Underneath all the details is a simple observation. Many professional people become so devoted to their work that they destroy their health—the true substance of their "personal chemistry." Once you understand that concept there are many paths to health; but I won't practice medicine on you. I'm not that kind of doctor. I am the kind of doctor that heals organizations, and there are things an organization can do to establish a healthy climate for health. That's why I advise data processing managers to set a good example for their employees by

1. Working regular hours *most* of the time
2. Taking time to eat properly, so as not to set a standard of working through or hurrying through lunch (or supper, if you're violating rule number 1)
3. Never rewarding people for working excessive hours or for skipping meals, but instead rewarding people for being sufficiently well organized to finish a normal day's work in a normal day

It's all too easy to adopt the pattern of work for work's sake or for the sake of how it looks to others. But you can break that pattern by reminding yourself that your body is your number-one piece of professional equipment. If it goes down, all the king's horses and all the king's men can't get it up and running again. In fact, I doubt whether even IBM's field engineers would do you much good.

What a Programmer Needs in Order to Change

Weinbergs' Law of Twins

Once upon a time, I wrote a book entitled *The Psychology of Computer Programming*. Although the book has made me rich and famous, the word *psychology* in the title makes many people consider me a psychologist. I'd better correct this gross mistake.

I have no certification as a psychologist. I have no degree in psychology. I can't cure a case of depression or even a mild case of kleptomania. In fact, when I went to college, I studiously avoided taking *any* psychology course or even being seen with a psychology professor.

Quite frankly, I always suspected that the whole field of psychology was 50 percent error and 50 percent fake. As I matured, however, I began to have more respect for the work of some psychologists. Eventually, I came to appreciate what a difficult job they have selling themselves to the public. After all, every bartender is an expert in human behavior, without any license, degree, course, book, or training.

Indeed, most of human behavior is ridiculously simple to predict. From meteorologists we learn that two-thirds of the time you can predict tomorrow's weather correctly by saying it will be the same as today's. This makes everyone an expert on the weather—with only 66 percent correct. Imagine how many experts there are in psychology, where we can predict 99 percent of human behavior—with a simple law called Weinbergs' Law of Twins.

Your psychology professors never taught you Weinbergs' Law of Twins, but you must forgive them. Nobody wants to give away professional secrets. Would you take psychology courses if you knew they covered only 1 percent of the subject and that you could learn the rest in one painless minute?

Like many truly great laws, this one had the most humble beginnings. The Weinbergs were sitting on the Number 44 bus, heading up Broadway in the gloom of a winter rush hour, when a haggard but pretty young woman boarded with eight children in tow.

"How much is the fare?" she asked the driver.

"Thirty-five cents for adults, and children under five ride free."

"Okay," she said, shifting one of the two tiniest she carried under her arms so she could reach her purse. She dropped two coins into the fare box and started with her entourage down the aisle.

"Wait just a minute, lady!" the driver commanded, as only a New York bus driver can. "You don't expect me to believe that all eight of them children is under five!"

"Of course they are," she said indignantly. "These two are four, the girls are three, the toddlers are two, and these little ones are one."

The driver was dumbfounded and apologetic. "Gee lady, I'm sorry. Do you *always* have twins?"

"Oh, no," she said, managing to straighten a wisp of brown hair. "Most of the time we don't have *any*."

And there it was, in a flash, to both of us at once. Most of the time, for most systems in the world, nothing of any significance happens. Indeed, if you look one minute and then look the next, most of the time you see almost exactly the same thing. For most systems of any kind, the best prediction you can make is that in the next instant of time they will be doing just what they were doing in the previous instant of time.

Needless to say, we were elated. Our fame was assured by the discovery of what had to become the most important of all laws, transcending the discoveries of any discipline, of mathematics, of philosophy itself. And then, just as suddenly as the elation had come, gloom descended. For although the new law was certainly important enough to carry the name Weinbergs' Law, it was, like an earlier Weinbergs' law, a law about the *frequency of twin births*! It could not, therefore, be given its proper name, Weinbergs' Law of Twins, for that name was already inscribed in the history of science.

We were heartbroken, so much so that we didn't tell anybody about our law for many years. When we finally screwed up the courage, our friends merely laughed. "Why don't be silly," they chided us. "There are any number of precedents you can follow. Why, just think of Newton's First and Second Laws of Motion."

And so it was that our chance for ascending to the Valhalla of Science was reborn. There, etched in some marble throne, are Weinbergs' Law of Twins and Weinbergs' Second Law of Twins. Leaving aside the fancy mathematics, in general systems terms the First Law of Twins says:

Among all births, twin births are pretty rare, and triplets are rarer still.

The Second Law—*our* Law—says:

Even though twin births are rare among all births, births themselves are almost infinitely rarer than no births at all.

As with Newton's laws of motion, the Second Law here, if we must say so ourselves, is by far the more important of the two, in spite of any implications of the word *second*. It is important because it does indeed predict 99 percent of human behavior, and about the same amount of the behavior of other systems as well. Consider the average woman in the United States. She lives to be 70.7 years and gives birth to 2.1 children. This means that on any day of her life, chosen at random, her chance of giving birth at all is less than .01 percent. (For men, of course, the odds are even lower.) On the other hand, if she does give birth on a certain day, her chance of having twins or better is about 1.5 percent. Therefore, the Second Law is at least 100 times more powerful than the first.

For some reason, though, we haven't become as famous as we expected. It seems that most people claim to have known this law already, though nobody can give reference to a publication in a respectable journal. Perhaps the problem is that people expect too much of a law. People want an explanation of social continuity, not just a law proclaiming its universality. Well, that's not as easy, as it turns out. If we're going to explain why most of the time nothing much happens, it will take a whole book, and then some.

That's a job Dani Weinberg has undertaken in our book *On the Design of Stable Systems,* so I won't repeat it here. Instead, I'll examine some of the consequences of social continuity for those who are trying to improve the way a professional programmer develops computer applications.

The First Law of Inertia

Once you understand that nonchange is the rule, and change the very rare exception, you begin to wonder: If nonchange is so universal, how does it happen that anything changes at all? This question is an excellent starting point for understanding change. You must begin to see change as something wonderful, rare, and worth observing. You must stop taking change for granted if you wish to master the art of productive change.

But people do take change for granted. If nonchange is the rule, and change is the exception, how can this be? Evidently, change is not so rare that it's foreign to us. When we understand the most common reasons for change—the reasons change isn't a rare experience—we're well along the path of mastering change.

Imagine that you are a professional golfer—one of the best. Let's say you are fourteenth on the money list, earning about $187,000 a year in prize money plus a comparable sum in endorsements and side bets. Imagine further that you have mastered your technique to the point that you can play with great consistency. In tournament after tournament, on course after course, you finish with a total score near par for four rounds.

Now if you examine winning golf scores over the past several decades, you'll discover that the winning scores have gradually become lower and lower. Some sportswriters attribute this change to easier courses. Some say it's improved equipment, or better technique, or higher prize money that allows the better players more chances to stay in the game and have a successful career. Actually, all these factors are involved, and perhaps many more subtle factors are involved as well.

But whatever the reasons, the trend is continuing. Therefore, if your game remains absolutely constant, what will happen to your professional career?

This year you won $187,000. What will you win next year? Obviously, if scores are improving, your average finish is going to be lower. Unless prize money increases, your income will decrease. Also, you'll win fewer bets and get fewer endorsements. In short, no matter how unchanging you can be, if your environment changes, your own situation will probably change.

If you drive a car straight down the street and the street changes into a pier, and if you don't change your speed or direction, your environment will change them for you. We call this the Law of Inertia: "Inability to change eventually leads to dramatic or catastrophic change."

The Second Law of Inertia

In a world where failure to change eventually leads to catastrophe, systems that don't learn to change gracefully don't last long. Systems that last have developed sophisticated techniques for resisting change or for steering change into more acceptable channels.

As an example, consider what happens when someone attempts to introduce a new technology to a person with an established skill. To keep clear of anyone's toes, let's stick to the example of the professional golfer. It's the off-season, and you've just won $187,000. You're having lunch with the representative of a sporting goods company who is trying to sell you a new and radically different set of clubs. Using these clubs, the representative claims, you can cut one stroke per round off your game. More than that, if you endorse the clubs, you won't even have to pay for them. Indeed, the company will pay *you* $10,000 to use them. What's your reaction?

If you're the normal person, you'll listen for a while and then refuse the offer. Who are they to tell you how to improve your game? Don't they know that you're fourteenth on the money list?

Or perhaps you're a truly open, innovative person, willing to give anything a try. You ask for a set of clubs and take them onto your home course early one morning to practice. The first thing you notice is that the clubs feel strange, unbalanced. Your swing is distorted and you start slicing. After a few holes, you've over-corrected the slice and hooked your tee shot into the creek. You hack your way around the course, secretly glad that it's too early for anybody to be out watching you. In the clubhouse, you total your card and find you've scored an 83! Eleven over par! Worse than that, your confidence is shaken and you suspect that your timing has been thrown off even if you go back to your regular clubs. You call the sales rep and say politely, "Thanks, but no thanks."

The sales rep argues that a little deterioration is to be expected in the beginning. For one season, or maybe only half a season, you'll lose a few strokes off your previous game, but soon you'll be under par again. To make the argument convincing, the rep lays out the results of last year's tournaments and demonstrates what a decrease of one stroke per round would have done for you. In three tournaments, it would have been enough to make you the winner. Overall, it would have raised your direct earnings from $187,000 to $430,000. Isn't that worth a little trouble at the beginning?

But you're not really listening. Instead, you're calculating what an increase of one stroke per round would have done: your earnings would have dropped from $187,000 to $45,000. Even worse, you wouldn't have won the two tournaments you did win, so you'd have lost most of your endorsements. Indeed, this sales rep wouldn't even be here talking to you if you hadn't won those two tournaments. And if you'd used these cockamamie clubs, you surely wouldn't have won anything.

If the sporting goods company knew their business, they wouldn't have come to you in the first place. Instead, they'd have picked some pro who's just been dropped from the tour for not making the cut in enough tournaments, or a young pro who hasn't yet made the tour at all. *Their* income isn't $187,000. In fact, their net is probably negative for the year. They will really appreciate the $10,000, but perhaps they'll appreciate the attention even more.

But most important, they aren't going to suffer a drop in income if their game falls off by a few strokes, so they've got little to lose by trying new clubs or any other innovation. Conversely, if they do improve by a few strokes, it means the difference between being a golfer and being a caddy.

Do I have to spell out the parallels with computer programming? Or with the way we usually try to introduce some new technique? Let me summarize what I've said about change in two laws of change:

1. People change when forced to change by changes in their environment. This is the First Law of Inertia.
2. When forced to change, people struggle to preserve the things that are most important to them at the expense of things that are less important. This is the Second Law of Inertia.

Romer's Rule

Which is the more powerful force of change, the First Law of Inertia or the Second Law of Inertia? Where do the biggest and longest-lasting changes originate? These questions have an interesting answer, first formulated by paleontologist Alfred Romer to explain the changes he found in the fossil record. How could it happen, Romer asked, that sea creatures would come out of the water and begin to breathe air and live on land, when they were so well adapted to the water and the air was poisonous to them?

Romer envisioned the situation in which conditions in the water were becoming crowded. Perhaps a lake was shrinking because of a dry turn in the climate. Perhaps new types of fish were beginning to beat the older varieties in the competition for food. Whatever the reason, there was limited food in the water, so any species that could obtain additional food from some other source would be favored over those that couldn't. Under such conditions, one species might accidentally adopt the practice of creeping or leaping out of the water for a few moments—holding its breath, so to speak—in order to nibble at the plants growing at the water's edge. From the point of view of the other fish, this species was moving into a fourth dimension. From its own point of view, it was temporarily moving out of its favored environment in order that it could permanently survive in that environment.

In short, our first land-crawling ancestors came out of the water in order to stay in the water. But once they made that first tiny step, the die was cast, and some of their descendants eventually reached the point where the land, not the water, was their primary environment. This, then, is Romer's Rule:

> The biggest and longest-lasting changes usually originate in attempts to preserve the very thing that ultimately changes most.

The world of data processing abounds with examples of Romer's Rule. Most companies started using computers in the first place not so their business would change, but so that their business would remain pretty much the same as it always had been. For instance, as the volume of transactions grows, old methods of transaction processing begin to collapse under the burden. The life of the business is threatened unless it can develop a method of coping with the increase. A computer is brought in—and sets in motion a chain of events as irreversible as that caused by the first fish creeping out of the water to nibble a fern.

In the light of Romer's Rule, the person who wants to manage the course of change will not fight the system's attempts to preserve itself but will harness those attempts to the desired course of change. The determination *not* to change is usually the most powerful force available. If you fight it directly, you are almost sure to lose. If you harness it to the changes you want, in such a way that the system will struggle to preserve what it values most, you have a reasonable chance of success. That is one of the great lessons of the past, whether applied to countries, companies, or co-workers.

The Changes in Programming Productivity

Let's bring these ideas closer to home. During the past three decades, winning golf scores have dropped a few strokes in several hundred (perhaps 1 or 2 percent), yet the entire professional game has been revolutionized. During that same period, the speed and capacity of computers has changed by *millions or billions.* What must those changes have done to the professional computer person—the programmer?

On the surface, there hasn't been that much change, which is why we hear a lot about human productivity not increasing. In 1979 I did an experiment with my IBM 5110 that convinced me that the lack of change in productivity is an illusion, at least in some cases. In 1956 I left school and went to work for IBM in San Francisco. I was allowed to play with the new 650 computer to teach myself programming, as there were no classes at that time. After a few practice problems, I was commissioned to teach a programming course to my colleagues, an experience that proved most educational —to me, if not to them. Then I had a chance to write my first real application program. Working with a young civil engineer, Lyle Hoag, I wrote a program to analyze hydraulic networks—the systems that serve the water needs of a city. Computers were so new that the application was a great innovation, worthy of publication—my first —in the *Journal of the American Water Works Association.*

Since that time, I've written hundreds of application programs and assisted on thousands more, almost all of which I've forgotten. But because that first one happened to result in publication, I can read about it more than twenty years later and get pretty reliable information about my productivity way back then.

Using my 5110 and programming in APL, I reproduced that application from the past in order to see if my productivity as a programmer had increased. In 1956, two of us worked more than four weeks full-time plus lots of overtime to write and test our system. In 1979, I produced version 2 of the program in about two and a half hours of work, an increase in productivity of over 200 times. That amounts to over 25 percent per year, which certainly exceeds the increases in any other labor-intensive occupation I know.

Of course, programming as a whole has not kept pace with this 25 percent annual increase, largely because we keep removing or driving our most productive people from the programming ranks. Also, this great improvement hasn't even kept pace with the increased speed and capacity of the computers themselves, so the ranks of programmers have swelled—wiping out the increased productivity of any outstanding old-timers who have remained. And larger numbers means more management, more communications loss, more overhead—all of which further reduce apparent productivity. Finally, our gargantuan investment in old software and software tools has acted as a dead weight that must be dragged aiong by each programmer in the quest of increasing quality or quantity of output.

None of this would be much of a problem if programmers were regarded in a different light. As one programmer expressed it to me, "Why isn't my manager satisfied with a 5 percent increase in my productivity each year? Her productivity hasn't increased at all in ten years."

I explained to him that a manager's productivity is measured in a different way—by the productivity of the people she manages. He then asked a very penetrating question: "Why, then, isn't my productivity measured in the same way—by the productivity of the programs I write?" Why indeed?

The programmer, like the manager, is not a direct producer, but an indirect one. If you don't understand the consequences of this observation, ask yourself which of the following two programmers you would consider better.

1. Dorothy, who now writes 110 lines of code in the same time she used to write 100 lines of code, but whose programs are exactly the same as they always were.
2. Herbert, who still takes the same amount of time to write 100 lines, but whose programs help the thousand clerks who use them increase *their* productivity by 1 percent.

When I rewrote the hydraulic network analysis program in 1979, I made numerous improvements, especially in the input and output formats, but these were not counted in my estimate of productivity increase. Yet the old program was used by hundreds of civil engineers—highly skilled and highly paid people who wasted many hours and made many costly mistakes because the old input format was tedious to prepare and the output format was hard to read.

Traditionally, however, most DP organizations have mentally classified the programmers along with the clerks, whose productivity is counted directly, not according to the productivity of their product. As a consequence, many programmers have responded to the pressure for productivity by doing just what this measure implies—increasing the amount of code rather than the quality of code.

In fact, real programming work is a combination of clerical and creative work, just as real management is. What's important in one organization at one time will be secondary at another time or in another organization. Thus programmers are not only being asked to produce more, but they are also being asked to decide what kind of "more" they should produce. These same pressures are felt by data-processing management, fed down from upper management, and passed along to the programmers after being translated into DP management's currently favored idiom. The new result is that programmers who sense they are more productive than they've ever been feel that their management:

1. Doesn't know what they want
2. Is pressuring for an increase in "productivity" even though they don't know what they mean by the word
3. Doesn't appreciate what has already been accomplished
4. Has put up most of the barriers that prevent the programmers from increasing productivity of any kind

What the Programmer Needs

By the First Law of Inertia we know that the programmer should feel the squeeze. By the Second Law we know that the programmer's response to the squeeze will depend on what's important for the programmer to preserve. Therefore, we must ask, "What do these changes threaten that the programmer values?"

Psychologists tell us that human beings have a hierarchy of needs. What this means is that certain needs are placed before other needs—until they are satisfied. Then they cease being needs and are replaced by the next level of needs in the hierarchy. For instance, the most crucial needs are physiological. If you're running out of air, you're not very interested in obtaining your manager's esteem. Generally, in today's developed societies, and particularly among programmers, there's not much motivational force in air, water, or food. The great rise in computational power has not really threatened any programmer with starvation, and legal obstacles prevent managers from threatening, "If you don't code faster, I'll suffocate you!" In other fields, if productivity doesn't increase faster, the management may be able to operate on the next level of the hierarchy—the level of security. It's certainly legal to say, "If you don't code faster, I'll fire you!" But will this approach produce the necessary motivation for change?

In today's business environment, the threat of firing is not very effective with most programmers. First, in many large organizations the threat is essentially hollow, for it's easier to put people in a corner and keep on paying them than it is to fire them. But even if firing is feasible, one glance at the "programmers wanted" ads will show you why the threat lacks conviction.

For more than twenty years, I've listened to forecasts of the demise of programming. Managers like to hear these forecasts because they know that if programming jobs were getting scarcer, programmers would be responsive to threats of firing. I lack the space to justify my own forecasts, but to the practical manager I offer this advice: "Don't wait for the decline in programming to solve your problems."

Actually, the threat of firing seems to carry more force than the want ads would suggest, but it's not because the programmer is worried about security. On the next level of needs is the need to belong to some social group. This is the need that's most threatened by the loss of a job. Many managers fret and moan about the "social life" at the office, not understanding that for many of their employees, this "social life" is all that stands between them and another job at a higher salary.

Having reached a relatively secure and comfortable existence, the average programmer is seeking to fulfill such higher needs, which the psychologists list as:

Belonging—being part of a group
Esteem—being highly regarded by others
Self-actualization—being highly regarded by oneself

These are the areas in which the programmer may be squeezed by the First Law of Inertia, so these are the areas the programmer will strive to preserve according to the Second Law of Inertia. Let's see them at work in cases from several of my clients.

CASE 1: *Money as a Measure of Esteem*

Manuel has been programming for five years and he can sense his increased programming powers. When a trainee comes to him with a problem, he realizes that he would write the program in one-third the time it takes the trainee. He is satisfying his need to belong because the trainee comes to *him*, which puts him in something of a father-of-the-family role. This same role satisfies his need to be esteemed, for the trainee obviously respects his skills. Finally, his private sense of his own powers satisfies his highest need—the need for self-actualization. He is doing something worthy and he knows he's good at it.

A few days later, Manuel happens to learn that the trainee is earning $30,000, compared to his salary of $40,000. The $40,000 is more than enough to satisfy his physical needs, and his job is certainly secure, but he feels uneasy. "Why," he thinks, "do I get only one-third more money when I'm at least three times as productive? Perhaps my manager doesn't appreciate my skill." His esteem is threatened, so he's motivated to do something about it.

He watches the newspaper to verify his feeling. He learns that nobody is paid three times as much just because they produce three times as much, which restores some of his esteem. He's learned that the value of salary differences is more symbolic than direct.

But he's also seen that the agency ads are promising well above $40,000 for someone with his experience, so not all his anxiety is relieved. He doesn't think of quitting, because all his friends work here, but he decides to raise the question of salary during his annual appraisal.

At the appraisal, Jean, Manuel's manager, is grouchy. She's been under pressure to raise productivity by introducing new methods and keeping the lid on personnel costs. She's planned a tiny raise for Manuel—less than she'd like to give—and she feels that she must justify giving such a small amount by telling him that he hasn't been adopting new methods. Besides, she has no way of measuring just how productive Manuel has been or could be if given a chance.

The pressure is on her because the great rise in computing power has also led to a rise in management expectations. Once we program something, the door opens and in march the users with the problems they really wanted to solve. As a result, much of Manuel's 25 percent annual productivity increase has been absorbed into more sophisticated applications for which he, as programmer, gets hardly any credit at all.

To make matters worse, Jean doesn't have time to examine Manuel's work personally to see whether he's actually using the new methods. Even if she did, she no longer has the technical skills that once earned her the promotion to this management job. Manuel knows this, so if Jean tries to criticize his work, he feels she's being unfair. Yet if she tries to praise the work, he'll discount the worth of her praise to his self-esteem. Certainly Manuel knows that Jean is no longer part of the group of programmers to which he belongs. By taking the management job, she's indicated that she doesn't value their comradeship any longer.

It's unlikely that such an appraisal meeting can be very satisfactory to either Manuel or Jean, which is probably why both will avoid the next one. If Manuel can avoid too much contact with Jean, he may remain satisfied with his job, especially if he maintains contact with his peers. If not, he'll soon be answering one of those ads or listening to a recruiter who got his name from a former employee who left three months ago. With an old friend as a bridge to a new job, Manuel's greatest fears are relieved, for he will immediately belong to a group in that new environment.

But the most important moral of this story is that nowhere was Manuel ever really motivated to adopt new methods to work more productively, at least by any management action. Indeed, every attempt by management to reach Manuel and provide motivation tended to work backward. Manuel might be motivated, but not to increase productivity. Instead, he might choose among the following as solutions to his work situation:

1. Leaving for a new job
2. Avoiding his manager's eye as much as possible
3. Working less to compensate for his "underpayment"

And even if Manuel really felt he needed more money, he's not likely to try to get it by increasing productivity. Instead, he may try such avenues as

1. Pushing for a management job
2. Taking on a little night work writing programs for the local CPA's minicomputer

Both of these approaches will actually lessen the productivity of Jean's organization—one through loss of an experienced person and the other through loss of that person's time and dedication.

CASE 2: *Technical Reviews as Motivators*

Now let's consider another approach to motivation. Muriel, like Manuel, was a pretty good programmer after five years, although she lacked confidence in herself. Consequently, she was quite worried when Claude, her manager, announced that he was introducing a system of formal code reviews. Because Muriel was the most experienced person on her project, her work was chosen for the first review. She was so nervous she couldn't sleep the night before. As she tossed and turned, she seriously considered calling in sick—and spending the day calling some of the numbers in the want ads.

In the end, Muriel came to work, mostly because she didn't want her friends to think she was a coward. As the review started, she began to realize her worst fears. Three rather serious bugs were brought up in the first round of comments. She wanted to defend herself, but she knew the others were right. Finally, she asked if she could terminate the review and have another chance to fix her code.

The review leader—who had been well prepared for his task —kindly but firmly explained that terminating the review was not Muriel's decision. Only the review group could decide, but he would poll them if she wished. She did, so the matter was discussed. To Muriel's surprise, she heard one reviewer say that if these bugs were all that was wrong with the program, then it was better than any program he had ever seen at this stage of development. She was even more surprised when the rest of the group agreed with that judgment and remarked on how much they had learned about new techniques from Muriel.

The review leader then gave the group a mild rebuke for starting the review in such a completely negative fashion, reminding them that Muriel was the first person on the project to have anything reviewed. Naturally, he said, she would be sensitive to criticism, not knowing just how good a program was expected of her. Finally, the group voted to continue the review. After another twenty minutes—in which a number of Muriel's techniques were praised—they terminated the review with a decision to accept the code after the three bugs were corrected and two additional tests were run successfully.

A month after this experience, Muriel was a student in one of my workshops, which is where she told me her story. She said that she would never forget the rest of that day following the review, though she could hardly remember anything specific about it at all. What she remembered most was what she described as a "glow" or "tingling feeling," and several people stopping by her cubicle to congratulate her on what they had heard was an outstanding piece of work.

Muriel's manager, Claude, who was in the same workshop, told me that he had chosen Muriel first because he knew her work was the best in the shop, but she never believed him when he tried to tell her. In one fell swoop, he had managed to satisfy all three of her highest needs—for a sense of belonging, for the esteem of her colleagues, and for her self-esteem.

During our discussions at the workshop, Muriel emerged as a staunch supporter of formal reviews. As she regaled the class with example after example from her own shop, it was hard to imagine her being afraid to come to work for her first review.

Ford's Fundamental Feedback Formula

In both of these cases, the managers were trying to accomplish the same thing—motivating the programmer to use new methods to work more productively and perhaps to help others work more productively. Yet one case was an utter failure and the other a complete success. Why the difference?

I believe the first manager failed because she thought that to manage change you must interact directly with the employee. Although direct intervention is sometimes the correct tactic, the effective manager works with a far broader spectrum of approaches. In particular, Muriel's manager was effective because he harnessed the social processes of the office to serve the organization's productivity goals.

To understand how this worked, let's use another metaphor. Lack of productivity is like pollution—something unwanted in people's output, like poisonous chemicals a factory is dumping in the river. Back in the 1920s Congress was investigating river pollution and invited Henry Ford, as a top industrialist, to testify. When Ford took the stand, he chided the Congress for wasting good tax money on complicated antipollution laws. "All you need," he said, "is one simple law to clear up all polluted rivers."

The members of the committee listened in disbelief and ultimately didn't follow Ford's advice. But if they had, there's no question but that Ford's law would have worked. You can judge for yourself, for what he proposed was this:

> Anyone can take any amount of water from any river for any purpose whatsoever, as long as they return the water *upstream* from where they took it out.

You see, people may be willing to drink other people's sewage, but they'll never be willing to drink their own. If they have to return their waters upstream, you can be sure that they'll do whatever is necessary to purify their output.

I believe that this principle is one of the most profound weapons in the management armory, so I've given it a name honoring one of the most profound managers of all time—Ford's Fundamental Feedback Formula. Simply put, Ford's Formula says:

> If you want people to change what they're doing, make sure they are fed back the consequences of what they're doing.

I believe that many of the problems we have in improving the productivity of programming stem from a failure of management to apply this principle. Many programmers—probably *most* programmers—work in environments in which they receive essentially no real feedback embodying the consequences of what they do. Lacking this feedback, they lack the motivation to attempt changes, and they also lack the information needed to make the *correct* changes.

In the light of Ford's Formula, we can understand the real difference between the cases of Manuel and Muriel. Manuel's manager, first of all, didn't know precisely what Manuel was doing, so her attempt to direct feedback was doomed to failure. Even had Manuel believed what she was saying, he had no real information to use to improve his productivity. Indeed, he might well have made things worse by attempting to follow her opinions about what he should and should not be doing.

Jean's method is very commonly used by programming managers. Jean came up through the ranks herself, and before officially becoming a manager she was put in charge of three trainees for more than a year. Working with the trainees, she applied the direct method with great success—so much success that she was promoted. But as manager of a group of experienced programmers, she couldn't successfully apply the same method she used with the trainees.

Jean thought she was using the same method, but she no longer had the information to feed back to Manuel. She didn't have time to examine everyone's work as she had when her total responsibility was three trainees. Not having time to examine actual work, she soon lost the competence to examine work even when she had the time. Moreover, she never had the competence, all by herself, to examine the work of experienced programmers and note everything good and bad about it. That was no shortcoming in Jean, however, because nobody in the installation was that much better than everyone else.

In Muriel's shop, the situation was much the same. Through the review procedures, however, Claude pooled the technical knowledge, giving a result that was superior to any one particular person's contribution. Moreover, the people doing the reviewing had adequate time. Each reviewer benefited directly by learning relevant things in each review, which easily repaid them for the time they spent and which spread good new techniques like wildfire. Through the review, the feedback was more relevant, more believable, and more complete than Muriel's manager, or any manager, could possibly have given.

There are many forms of technical reviews, and there are many other ways a manager can harness social forces in the service of Ford's Fundamental Feedback Formula. I chose to make an example of reviews because I believe reviews are the one most immediately productive step any programming manager can take *today*. Even more important, without reviews there is no way in the world a programming manager can be confident in the implementation of *any* productivity technique. I have been in dozens of shops that bragged about their implementation of structured programming, special testing tools, new forms of documentation, new standards, or what have you. In most of these shops, an on-the-ground investigation showed that in spite of the manager's illusions, the programmers simply were not using the techniques to any great extent. And, lacking reviews, the manager had no reliable way of dispelling this illusion.

Summary

1. Most of the time change doesn't happen.
2. The reason change doesn't happen is that many forces are actively working to keep things stable.
3. To direct change toward productive channels, you must understand the forces that work for stability.
4. When people do change, it's because their environment is changing, so they change even if they stay the same; their environment is changing, so they change one thing to preserve something even more important to themselves.
5. The biggest change ultimately results from trying to preserve the thing that changes.
6. The things people are trying to preserve are ranked in the following hierarchy of needs:
   Physical needs
   Security
   A feeling of belonging
   Esteem from others
   Self-esteem or self-actualization
7. In today's environment, few programmers are motivated by physical needs or security.
8. If people are fed back the results of what they're doing, so that they feel what's good and what's bad, they will see to it that they change to increase the good and decrease the bad.
9. The manager's job is not necessarily to feed back this information, but to arrange matters so that the feedback takes place, reliably and regularly.
10. Because programmers' physical needs and security needs are

pretty well satisfied, the more successful management strategies will be arrangements that work to satisfy the higher needs —in particular, social needs.

11. Technical reviews by a programmer's peers are one outstanding example of a strategy that harnesses these higher needs to feed back reliable information on programmer performance.

12. There are many forms of technical reviews, and they can be adapted to any organization; but without technical reviews of some sort, you're probably wasting most of the money you spend on other productivity techniques.

Fooling with Rules

"**W**hat is green, has wheels, and grows around the house?"

"I give up. What's the answer?"

"Grass . . . I lied about the wheels."

By this little twist, one of Poul Anderson's heroes sends a wicked giant into a rage and defeats him in a riddling contest. Would he have defeated you? Does that mean you are a wicked giant? Or does it mean you're just like the typical computer programmer?

Programmers are terribly bothered when they must play a game without knowing all the rules. When they know there *are* rules, some of which are not stated, most programmers will work that much harder—trying to discover the hidden rules. But once they feel there are no rules, or that the rules can be arbitrarily changed, programmers tend to get hostile and quit the game.

Psychologists would say this behavior indicates a strong need for a feeling of control. Such feelings influence the kinds of jobs programmers seek and keep, their desire or lack of desire to assume management responsibilities, their entire attitude toward styles of management, their feelings about team programming and technical reviews, and many other aspects of the programming life-style. One reason programmers like to play in rule-bound situations is that they're good at it: People who aren't successful in such situations usually don't go into the programming business. If you're managing programmers and you want the workers to be happy, you have to establish an environment in which the rules are clear and known to all. You can be sure they'll play by any rules you set down clearly. Be careful, though. If some rules aren't carefully thought out, you may get surprising results. For instance, if you mandate that a programmer producing more lines of code gets more salary, programmers will react like squirrels with nuts and start producing hoards of code. If the game is changed so that producing fewer lines of code results in a higher salary, they'll happily switch styles and produce fewer lines of code.

I once talked to a programmer who was quite content working for a manager whom I considered an awful person. I asked this programmer how he could tolerate working for a guy who seemed to be completely arbitrary and willing to do anything to anybody to advance his career. The programmer explained that this behavior was exactly what made the situation tolerable. The manager wasn't arbitrary, as I had thought, but he lived by one very simple rule: He never stabbed anybody in the back unless it would advance his career. If you kept out of his path, so he couldn't benefit by knifing you in some way, then he never gave you any trouble. This made him perfectly predictable, at least for this particular programmer, who had no aspirations to advance to higher levels of management. The programmer was quite content—he had a set of rules that he understood only too well.

Recently, my wife and I were invited to study the psychological effects of new software tools on a large programming organization. There were many complaints, large and small, about one glitch or another in the software tools, but there was only one truly violent complaint that we heard from everyone: The systems group maintaining the tools changed the way the tools worked at arbitrary times, without any advance warning.

The programmers got livid when they discussed this behavior. Their anger can be easily understood in terms of their need and desire to be in a rule-bound situation. It would have been acceptable to them if rules changed, if only they were notified in advance. It would have been fine if rules changed, if only they were given reasons related to higher rules. But arbitrary and capricious rule changes by the systems group were completely unacceptable to everyone we interviewed.

As programmers advance in their careers, they do grow more sophisticated in what they consider to be rules. For example, young programmers are often enraged by customers changing specifications in the middle of a programming job. As they gain experience, programmers begin to deduce a higher-level rule: Customers *always* change the specifications in the middle of a programming job.

Having captured the essence of the matter in this larger rule, programmers are able to work with customers who change their minds. They get annoyed but not outraged. Many new tactics become available once programmers protect themselves against erratic behavior by bringing it within the bounds of rules. When the same behavior occurs outside of the rules, it leads to nothing productive.

Much like children testing parents or pets testing masters, programmers may throw tantrums any time a new set of rules is introduced. But if the rules are explicit, programmers soon adapt and work out new patterns of success within the new rules. If standards are added to the standards manual with a lot of fanfare, for example, programmers will initially scream and shout. If they notice after a while that the standards are enforced regularly, most programmers will follow the standards. On the other hand, if they find that the standards are not being enforced, then they induce a higher-level rule that says: Those rules (standards) don't really count ("I lied about the wheels"). It's then easy to ignore the standards that don't really count. Everyone is comfortable, because the rule by rule is restored. Over the centuries, programmers have adopted rules from other areas of life and have developed many of their own. Here's a list of ten of my favorites, which we might call Weinberg's Precious Programming Principles:

1. Standards aren't standard.
2. There's always one more bug, even after that one is removed.
3. Anything that can happen will happen, unless your test plan provides for it to happen.
4. When someone points a finger at some part of the code, look

somewhere else for the trouble—most likely where the other three fingers are pointing.

5. An ounce of prevention is worth a pound of cure, but management won't pay a penny for it.
6. Specifications, design, and coding can be done at any speed—only debugging takes time.
7. There is no code so big, twisted, or complex that maintenance can't make it worse.
8. Everyone talks about documentation, but nobody ever does anything about it.
9. You may run short of hardware, but you'll never run short of hardware salespeople.
10. Every programmer has at least ten personal principles, but only one programmer in ten thousand is willing to take the trouble to write down even one.

I know that rule 10 is true from talking to hundreds of programmers. Programmers have rules because they love rules. They particularly like meta-rules—rules about rules, like rule 1. Meta-rules constitute a favorite programmer game, but like any recursive game it must come to an end. I learned the ultimate in meta-rules when I visited a client looking for the source of some management difficulties. One programmer seemed calm and happy amid the widespread turmoil. I asked him how he survived, and if he could help others to cope with the situation.

"Oh, it's simple," he said, "there's only one rule around here."

"What's that?" I asked.

"The only rule here is that there are no rules here."

With a rule like that, everything was explained, and he was perfectly comfortable. Perhaps he had the right idea. Or perhaps it was grass, after all—the kind without wheels.

All I Want
Is a Little Respect!

In an interview with *Computerworld*, James Martin told a story about a government airline. He described how, if you are a passenger and

> you are exceptionally insulting to the air hostess, they put you on a blacklist. And that blacklist is then used so that when you try to make a booking on the airline again, the computer refuses you a seat.
>
> At the terminal I was shown how to display the blacklist. The amusing thing was that many of the people on the blacklist were people whose names you would know! I wonder if that would happen in a profit-making airline.

The first thing that caught my eye about this anecdote was Jim's contrasting a government airline with a profit-making airline. A lot of the privately owned lines in the United States have been reporting losses recently. When I lived in Switzerland, I learned that Swissair—which is completely government-owned—was the most consistently profitable airline in the world.

Another thing I learned in Switzerland was from a friend who owns one of the best restaurants in Geneva. One evening, while enjoying our usual supreme meal, we were disturbed by a gang of rowdy drunks two tables away. After several utterly courteous attempts to quiet them, my friend gave up. He personally apologized to the other diners for his inability to control such rude buffoons. Later that evening, after the restaurant had emptied, he confided to me that the one thing he hated most about the restaurant business was abusive drunks. In his many years as head waiter, and then as proprietor, he had never learned an effective way of dealing with them once they were in the restaurant. But, he confided, I could be sure that this particular bunch of hooligans would never again grace his premises. His wife, who took reservations, kept a blacklist of all similar churls. If they phoned for reservations, they were politely informed that no space was available.

The Swiss have a highly developed sense of appropriate behavior as it concerns the comfort of other people in public places. The English, too, have this sense—at least in England. But when they are away from their tight little island, the English can be even more rude than Americans. That's why, when I have a choice, I never fly on English or American airlines.

But perhaps it's unfair to paint with a single brush all citizens of two great nations. Jim did say that "many of the people on the blacklist were people whose names you would know." Perhaps the operational factor is not nation of origin but some kind of international status. Perhaps "famous" people feel that when they are rude, it's somehow less offensive to their fellow travelers?

Jim's mysterious airline could well be Swissair. I've never seen a Swiss who was terribly impressed with famous people. I'm sure that Swissair wouldn't be the least afraid of losing profits because it bumped a few celebrities off its passenger list. My restaurant friend certainly wasn't afraid to blacklist some of Geneva's famous louts, who might well have been U.N. dignitaries! People didn't come to his restaurant to see celebrities, but to enjoy exceptional food in pleasant surroundings.

All of which leads to the question: What's wrong with using the computer to blacklist people who make other people miserable? Jim seems to imply that regardless of whether it's wrong, it's a stupid business tactic—especially because so many of the boors are celebrities. Perhaps I've been spoiled by living in Switzerland, but when I'm on a long flight, I couldn't care less about celebrities. What I want is fellow passengers who are quiet and don't smoke in the non-smoking section.

But my view is rather limited and prejudiced. For those who are taking a once-in-a-lifetime vacation, perhaps putting up with offensive behavior is a small price to pay for the thrill of being seated across the aisle from a Hollywood star or one of the great minds of computing. In fact, without the offensive behavior, perhaps travelers wouldn't have any way of knowing just how famous their fellow passenger was!

I suppose I shouldn't be too hard on celebrities. We live in a rude society. In crowded conditions, it seems difficult to receive the simple respect that is the right of any ordinary person. Many of us, out of frustration, seek professional respect as a substitute for the social kind.

When I was a child, I was often treated as something less than a human being. This kind of treatment warped my thinking in several ways. It made me obsessed with seeking respect through my professional work. "After all," I reasoned, "if I'm the best programmer around, they'll have to treat me decently." I did achieve some professional success, but it never really made up for those childhood deficiencies. For one thing, no matter how good I was, I was never perfect and never indispensable, so nobody *had* to respect me.

But even when people did appreciate my good work and treated me decently, I still wasn't satisfied. What I really wanted was simple personal respect. I said to myself, in effect, "They don't really respect me as a person; they respect me because of the good work I do."

Eventually, I came to understand that what I truly wanted was to be able to respect *myself*. Nobody else could give me that, though other people had been able to take it away. When I finally was able to treat myself courteously, I found that I got along much better with airline attendants—and they don't even know anything about my professional accomplishments!

I also feel that I now have a better understanding of rude behavior, even when it is directed at me. Rude people, at the time they're being rude, have very little respect for *themselves*. We all feel that way sometimes, as when we are sitting cooped up on a long flight. But some people are that way almost all the time, and they're the ones who go on my blacklist.

There are many reasons why celebrities may feel little respect for themselves. They may have sought success, as I did, to make up for childhood abuse. Or, having found fame, they may be acutely sensitive to the discrepancies between their admirers' dreams and their own inner realities.

If you're good at your chosen profession, you'll have to confront such facts about yourself. Because of the way our socioeconomic system rewards professional success, it's all too easy to believe that outward success equals inner worth. But part of you is never fooled. As the discrepancy grows between your inner feelings of worth and your outer trappings of success, the tension will spill over onto the airline hostess. Or onto anyone else who happens to be witness to your distressing secret.

So don't worry too much about whether you're on the airline's computerized blacklist. Worry about whether you're on your own!

The Butterfly and the Buttercup: A Fable

Once upon a time, a butterfly came upon a buttercup growing alone on a grassy hill. The butterfly said, "You are the most beautiful butterfly I have ever seen, for the delicacy of your wings is a sight to behold."

The buttercup replied, "No other flower that I have known has such a free spirit as you, for your motion seems almost independent of the breezes." And so they fell in love.

A beetle resting on a nearby leaf observed the blossoming romance and called out to the lovers, "You ninnies, don't you know that members of different species cannot produce fertile offspring. Open your eyes and be rational about what you are doing."

But the butterfly and the buttercup were so much in love that their ears as well as their eyes were closed, and they did not hear a word of the beetle's advice. Consequently, they remained happily—though childlessly—in love for the remainder of their summer's life. The beetle, on the other hand, laid 38,312 eggs—8,729 of which hatched—in the next few years. Eventually, the beetle was squashed under the foot of a young

girl who was climbing the hill to look at the butterflies and butter-
cups.

MORAL: It's still better to be a barren butterfly or a battered buttercup than a brilliant, bountiful beetle.

IN OTHER WORDS: It's well nigh impossible for those who are motivated by productivity to understand those who are motivated
by quality—and vice versa.

Part IV

Is It Possible
to Think More Effectively?

Why Don't People Think?

A thought-provoking letter I received from David Flint of London begins:

> I suspect that the greatest disability from which SP [structured programming] suffers is the title of Dijkstra's original letter. Ever since people have supposed that simply by avoiding GOTO's they are performing structured programming and that they have improved their code. I was very struck by this when attempting to explain the SP concepts to other programmers and analysts in the Post Office.
>
> In my view the key to SP is not that programs should be structured, everything has a structure, but that they should be *well-structured*. People resist this because it sounds subjective and because it is more difficult than simply banishing GOTO's. Programmers, at least in commercial shops, are too eager to code and too reluctant to think—perhaps you should write an article on why this is so and what might be done about it. (Actually the causes are fairly obvious I think.)

I was with David all the way in this, up to the word *obvious*. I learned in the study of mathematics to beware of the word *obvious*, or *obviously*. It's a word designed to lull your thinking to sleep, which is just what we don't want to do. So here's a good rule for you—better perhaps than "eliminate all GOTO's":

Whenever you spot a "lullaby word," wake up!

Daniel Freedman and I have listed several pages of lullaby words in our *Handbook of Walkthroughs, Inspections, and Technical Reviews*. We use them as triggers when we're reading/reviewing specifications. They include such lovelies as: *all, all the time, every, may, only, same, should, too, will, certainly, therefore, clearly, obviously,* or *as any fool can plainly see*. The existence of such lullaby words in our language suggests some of the reasons David might have been hinting at why people don't think:

1. Somebody doesn't want them to think and is writing or speaking in such a way as to discourage thinking.
2. Nobody cares whether or not they think, but our habits of speech easily discourage thinking by making us sound very sure of ourselves when we may not be.

Why would language discourage us from thinking? Well, most of the time (outside of programming, certainly) thinking gets you into a lot of trouble. In most work environments, you're risking your job if you think very much, because work has been routinized. Thinking is believed to be a privilege of management, like a rubber plant next to your credenza.

Even in our private life, thinking is expensive. If you had to think about each bite of food you ate, or each time you crossed the street, you'd have little time for anything else. So you routinize your life in order to avoid thinking and save your time for other things —possibly for thinking about things that *require* thinking.

The same applies to programming. If we do happen to find some simple rule that always works and avoids the necessity for thinking, then we should apply that rule. Save the thinking for where it's needed.

For example, PL/I and COBOL allow the use of abbreviations

for certain keywords, but the abbreviations are optional. That means that each time you code one of these words, you might have to think about whether to use the abbreviated or unabbreviated form. Although you can muster arguments on both sides, it really doesn't matter much as long as you do one thing or another consistently with a particular keyword. Therefore, I always eliminate unnecessary thinking by deciding once and for all whether to abbreviate a particular keyword. Consequently, I never spell out CORRESPONDING or ENVIRONMENT, and I always spell out CHARACTER and PICTURE. It's a stupid habit, but it serves a purpose.

Of course, if I were coding some material as part of a system that had a different standard for those keywords, I'd willingly adjust my habits. But it would cost me some effort. Some of my thought would have to be diverted to remembering which system to follow. Naturally, I would appreciate having a system that spared me the choice, but I'm not going to waste any more valuable thought bemoaning its absence.

This brings up another reason why people don't like to think:

3. Thinking is tiring and may prevent other thinking.

When a programmer first starts to write structured programs, a lot of thought-saving habits have to go out his or her window. ("This is the way I write a loop," "This is the way I handle a three-way decision.") In the past these habits have been thought-saving, and it will cost thought to replace them with other habits. During the transition, all we feel is the extra thought and very little of the thought-saving.

But the "no GOTO" rule is actually another thought-saving habit (for me at least). When I find myself starting to write a GOTO, I use it as a trigger word rather than a lullaby word. I say to myself: "Weinberg, you've gotten into a lot of extra thinking in the past when you unthinkingly wrote a GOTO in similar situations. So why not think a little now and perhaps save a lot of thinking later, when you'll need it."

All of the other rules of structured programming—or of any good programming style—are this type of trigger rule. They say: "When you recognize this situation, stop sleeping and start thinking."

You can't operate on full consciousness all the time, even when you're doing something as dangerous as driving a car. So you accumulate a set of triggers to wake you up when things are getting dangerous. When you are driving, the triggers are such things as red and yellow lights, sirens, balls rolling into the street, children playing, or drivers ahead weaving from side to side.

In programming, there are triggers in the code, such as GOTO statements, tangled IF-THEN-ELSE logic, homologous parts that don't fit, garbled interfaces, and any code that seems to require more comment than code.

In our workshops, we pass out "trigger buttons" to participants who need to learn to trigger on certain words they utter that get them into trouble—words that they use to lull themselves or others to sleep. For instance, one of our favorite buttons is

THERE'S NO WAY.

Obviously (!), when you utter this you're saying, in effect, "There's no sense thinking about that, since it's impossible." When we hear "There's no way," we immediately award a button that the perpetrator has to wear until learning not to utter this lullaby phrase—or at least learning to catch the phrase as it emerges and use it as a thought trigger.

Another favorite lullaby phrase on our buttons is

WHAT CAN POSSIBLY GO WRONG?

This leads directly to the second part of David's letter:

> For your religion may I suggest "Skeptical Design"? The key concept being that you should examine your assumptions and designs as you proceed. As your first sacred text I suggest Bertrand Russell's advice: "Whatever you believe; do not *altogether* believe it." Russell had rather larger questions in view, of course.

"Skeptical Design" is a super name for the new programming religion, though Russell would probably spin in his grave to hear his advice used as a sacred text. Next time you're particularly satisfied with the design you've just completed, don't ask yourself *"What* can possibly go wrong?" but instead ask "What *can* possibly go wrong?"

And, of course, that leads to perhaps the most important reason of all that people don't think:

4. If I think about it too much, I might discover something wrong with it, and then where will I be?

Once again, this isn't entirely a stupid idea. For dozens of years, in schools, we're taught that "if the teacher doesn't catch it, it isn't wrong." So why make trouble for ourselves, when we know the teacher won't really have time to look at our work?

The problem is that computer programming bears very little resemblance to schoolwork. The "teacher"—the computer—looks at *all* of the work, and whatever is wrong is magnified hundreds or thousands of times. In school, it pays to bury your head in the sand —most of the time—so why should we expect people to behave otherwise when they're programming computers?

In sum, I've come up with four "obvious" reasons why people don't think:

1. Somebody wants them not to think.
2. Nobody cares whether or not they think.
3. Thinking too much may destroy the brain for other purposes.
4. We never learned to think in school.

Obviously, there's no way this list can possibly be wrong or incomplete. Want to take up the challenge?

Understanding the Professional Programmer

What Kind of Thinker Are You?

$\mathbf{H}$ere's a problem called the *Island's Puzzle* that has been much discussed as a measure of different styles of thinking. It was originally published by Robert Karplus around 1970 and has been used in training teachers to recognize different problem-solving styles. For college students, it may be quite a challenge, but for professional data-processing people, it should be quite a snap. Or should it? Have a go at it, but be careful. Write down your answers and reasoning, then look at my notes and see how you react to them.

The Islands Puzzle

The puzzle is about islands A, B, C, and D in the ocean. People have been traveling among these islands by boat for many years, but recently an airline started in business. Carefully read the clues about possible plane trips at present. The trips may be direct or include stops and plane changes on an island. When a trip is possible, it can be made in either direction between the islands. You may make notes or marks on the map to help use the clues.

First Clue: People can go by plane between islands C and D.

Second Clue: People cannot go by plane between islands A and B, even indirectly.

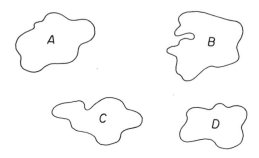

Use these two clues to answer question 1. Do not read the next clue yet.

Question 1: Can people go by plane between islands B and D? Yes____ No____ Can't tell from the two clues____ Please explain your answer.

Third Clue: (Do not change your answer to question 1 now.) People can go by plane between islands B and D.

Use all three clues to answer questions 2 and 3.

Question 2: Can people go by plane between islands B and C? Yes____ No____ Can't tell from the three clues____ Please explain your answer.

Question 3: Can people go by plane between islands A and C? Yes____ No____ Can't tell from the three clues____ Please explain your answer.

Notes on the Islands Puzzle

1. The problem statement says a trip "may be direct or include stops." Evidently, the terminology in this puzzle is different from standard airline terminology, as a direct flight may include stops. I'd better be careful—there may be other terms I don't understand.

2. I know a lot about air travel. Can I use any of that knowl-

edge in this puzzle, in view of the possible difficulty in terminology? Perhaps I know more about air travel than the creator of the puzzle, in which case I might see solutions that person couldn't see. That happens often when I work with travel agents. They're supposed to know a lot, but I've travelled much more than they, to many different parts of the world.

3. The first clue is straightforward enough—you can look in the *Airline Guide* and see that planes go from C to D. But the second clue looks suspicious. How can you see that you cannot go from one place to another? What can be the source of this kind of information? There must be a reasoning process involved, such as:

a. Nobody is allowed to fly to island A, either because there is no airport or because there are legal restrictions, or some such thing.
b. The travel agent has checked and hasn't been able to find a way.
c. There may be a way, but the travel agent thinks that layovers will be too long (this has happened to me often) and so just says it's "impossible."
d. There may be restrictions, such as quarantines, that don't allow anyone starting in B to end up in A, if they go by plane.

4. There are lots of other possibilities, but 3(d) made me look again at the statement of the clue: "People cannot go by plane between islands A and B, even indirectly." That definitely sounds like a contagious disease problem, or perhaps a political problem. If so, there are usually ways around it—bribes, vaccination certificates, letters of introduction from high government officials, submission to body search, or whatever. So although we don't have nearly enough information, we do have good reason to suspect the source of our clues. They may not know; they may misunderstand; they may have motives for misleading us. There's a lot more here than meets the eye.

5. As to question 1, we certainly don't have enough information in the two clues so far. We do know that planes can go to D, but perhaps planes cannot go to B at all. Still, that's pretty unlikely. I was once told that we couldn't fly to Maria Island in Tasmania, so we rented a plane and flew there. B looks like the biggest of the

islands. It might be mountainous, but so was Maria Island, and we found a little flat field to land in. Still, best to be safe and say "Can't tell from the two clues" even though there are many other clues than the things labeled "clues"—size of islands, size relative to distances, knowledge that there was boat travel (we took pontoon boats out to the reef islands), information about lack of knowledge of our informant, and so on.

6. Let's look at the third clue. Aha! Does this mean that one could always go from B to D, or that there is now new service? In the first instance, our informant wasn't very thorough not to tell us that. In the second, we've learned that things can change rapidly with this island airline. So it's a clue full of information.

7. In trying to answer question 2, we could be in danger if things have changed on the airline schedules, as clue 3 might imply. If they haven't, you are likely to be able to make it from B to C via D, but there could be quarantine restrictions and the like. The answer I think I'd better give is "Can't tell from the 3 clues." I don't even know which three clues the question is referring to, or if earlier clues are still valid, if they ever were.

8. As to question 3, we still don't even know if A is served by planes at all, yet we still might be able to rent one. If clue 2 was absolutely true, and was still valid after the airline had changed its schedule or after the travel agent had learned more, then I suppose you could conclude that going from A to C by plane was impossible. But that's not been my experience in traveling all over the world, so I'd certainly not want to say "no." On a probability basis, "yes" seems likely. If my life depended on giving the right answer, I'd have to say "can't tell." But if my job depended on getting from A to C, I sure wouldn't give up on the basis of what I've seen so far. I think I'd call a charter company and perhaps call another travel agent. If experience means anything, I'd probably find a flight from A to C and get a saving on my fare as well.

Reactions

The real question is this: "How did you feel about my analysis?"

I felt you were pulling my leg.
I felt you missed the point of the question.

I felt I missed the point of the question.

I felt you were right in approach, but wrong in reasoning.

I felt that your approach and reasoning made as much sense as the intended reasoning of the people who made up the problem.

I felt that all of the above were true, and false as well.

I felt that none of the above were true.

I felt that I wouldn't mark any answer to this stupid question.

I never allow myself to have feelings, especially about multiple-choice questions and puzzles.

I'm not sure what the point of all this is, except to joggle my thinking and yours about some of the things we take for granted. Especially how we take school as a model of life, when indeed life is infinitely more complex than school puzzles—even those intended to show how to think better in real life.

Someone has suggested that if you get the Islands Puzzle "right," you may be a good programmer, whereas if you did it more or less the way I did, you may be a good systems analyst (though not necessarily a bad programmer). As for me, I've learned over two decades that the number-one problem of both analysts and programmers—as well as their managers—is that they assume too much. They especially assume that they know what kind of problem they're working on—that it's a *puzzle* and not a *problem*.

Is It Concentration
or Compulsion?

Every profession has its secrets. Although ours must be *kept* secret, any secret from another profession appeals to our prurient nature. And of all the secrets, medical secrets have to be the juiciest. Unlike most people, I'm blessed with a brother-in-law, Marvin, who's a doctor, and a rather cynical one at that. One of the great secrets of medicine, Marvin assures me, is that 90 percent of all illness cures itself—with absolutely no intervention from the doctor. Because of this great secret, all the doctor needs to do is avoid harming the patient. Well, almost all. A successful doctor must also convince the patient that something is being done to cure the disease—something that could only come from the doctor's vast store of esoteric medical knowledge. Otherwise, there would soon be doctors on the breadlines.

The reason that 90 percent of all illness cures itself lies in the wisdom of the body. Although "wisdom" sounds mysterious, it's merely a poetical summary of the end result of thousands of generations of destructive testing carried on in thousands of millions of parallel replications, each lasting several decades. Most of those generations and tests were without benefit of modern medicine, so any body design that didn't have the wisdom to cure itself was summarily removed from the population. Each of us, after all, is the direct descendant of innumerable unbroken lines of survivors.

Unfortunately, this little medical secret isn't much help to computer people. As we know, there's very little, if any, "wisdom of the program." Each computer program has few if any ancestors. Whatever testing it has survived has been in its own short lifetime, so there's hardly been the time or space to perform hundreds of generations of thousands of millions of tests. That's one of the reasons computer programming is a much more demanding profession than medicine. And why we'll never be on breadlines.

Being in a demanding profession, the computer programmer needs all possible help from other professions. And even though the big secret of medicine won't help much, Marvin has taught me a few others that you just might be able to use. First of all, there's penicillin. Of the 10 percent of illnesses that don't cure themselves, penicillin or some other antibiotic handily dispatches another 90 percent. Contrary to popular belief, though, antibiotics alone aren't sufficient. They must be used properly, and that's where the doctor comes on stage.

For instance, indiscriminate popping of penicillin pills every time you have a cold can cause real harm. First off, the cold is one of the 90 percent of illnesses that will cure itself, so the penicillin does no good whatsoever. It might be of psychological assistance, but an inert pill would do that. Penicillin, in any case, is not inert, which means that although it's not affecting the cold, it is affecting other things. At the very least, it's affecting your body's sensitivity to penicillin, so someday when you really need some, it may have little or no effect. Even worse, it may provoke an allergic reaction.

Another common medical problem with penicillin is just the opposite of indiscriminate use. Perhaps because of all the warnings about the dangers of popping pills, people frequently stop taking their antibiotic pills too soon. Rather than complete the prescribed course of treatment, they stop if the most obvious and uncomfortable symptoms don't quickly disappear. In the case of bacterial infections, these symptoms may remain even though the offending organisms are being brought under control. But if the treatment stops too soon, the disease springs back. And this time, it's probably resistant to the antibiotic.

Do you see the parallel with programming? When attacking a tough problem, have you ever given up a promising line of attack prematurely—merely because you had to invest too much concentrated effort before seeing any definite results? Most programmers are familiar with this bitter experience. That's why they're able to concentrate on one problem to the exclusion of all worldly concerns. Show me the programmer who's never worked through a coffee break, and I'll show you a mediocre programmer. Show me a programmer who's never complained about being distracted from an important train of thought, and I'll show you a programmer's corpse.

For the moment, though, allow me to distract you from the question of concentration. I want to share another of Marvin's medical secrets. Actually, Marvin is not a mere M.D. but a psychiatrist. (No, that's not the secret.) Of all the medical gossip, none is more fascinating than the stories about crazy people. This story, however, is not about crazy people, but about psychiatrists—who everyone knows can't possibly be crazy, though they may not be very bright.

Once a month, Marvin drives down to the state mental hospital to consult with the staff on their most intransigent cases. This kind of consulting is his easiest work, Marvin says, because he really doesn't have to know any medicine or psychiatry at all. Whenever they bring out one of their tough cases, Marvin merely asks them what treatment they've been using. If they say treatment A, he tells them to switch to treatment B. If they tell him B, he says switch to A. Oh, he surrounds all this with suitable mumbo jumbo (doctors are the greatest suckers for their own medicine), but the principle is simple: Whatever they've been doing, tell them to stop and do something different.

It's easy to see why Marvin's system works. Because he's a consultant, the only cases he sees are the problems the hospital doctors aren't solving by themselves. Therefore, he concludes, the one thing he knows for sure is this: Whatever they're doing isn't right. They've become stuck on one approach and can't get off. Only because they're paying him a lot of money does this system work to get them unstuck. If he's so expensive, he must know what he's doing!

You'll notice, if you're a good programmer, that you already know this secret too. Are there programmers with souls so dead they never worked two days on a problem, only to get unstuck by an accidental hint from a colleague? Or even from a random interruption or accident? Yes, there's much the professions could learn from one another, if they only shared secrets.

But even more can be learned if we examine a profession's *collection* of secrets, side by side. For instance, consider these two we've just exposed:

1. Don't give up the treatment too soon.
2. Don't stick with one treatment too long.

Well, perhaps there's a reason, after all, that doctors make so much money. The secret of their secrets lies not in the secrets themselves, but in knowing when to apply each one. Maybe it's not *know-how* we're paying for, but "know-when."

In programming, too, most of our secrets come in complementary or contradictory pairs. If we practice just one, we get clobbered by the other. One way we fail as programmers is to be unable to concentrate on a problem until it cracks. Another road to failure is to be so obsessed with a problem that we miss some "obvious" solution.

There's one other lesson I've learned from Marvin—a lesson about what it means to be crazy. Psychiatrists didn't really begin to understand crazy people until they began to study "normal" people. For the most part, it seems, "crazy" behavior is just "normal" behavior carried to extremes.

I believe that this lesson, too, applies to programmers and to all sorts of would-be problem solvers. Our worst problem-solving behavior is merely our best behavior carried beyond its useful range. Carried too far, concentration turns to compulsion. Versatility turns to vacillation. The line separating the best problem solvers from the worst is perhaps much finer than we think, which should encourage the worst and provide a few sobering moments for the best. As Will Rogers once remarked about monkeys, "The reason we think they're so funny is that they're so much like us."

Can a Brain Be Unhealthy?

I'm not the kind of person who hangs out in nightclubs. The last nightclub I can remember was in Miami Beach in 1957, when I was attending the IBM Hundred Percent Club. There were several memorable events that night, but only one is suitable for printing—and I'm not so sure about that one, either, but I need it to make a point.

I recall the stand-up comic in the spotlight, his immaculate tuxedo in no way concealing his inner sleaziness. After warming the audience with some rather gross remarks, he stopped, pulled himself into an upright posture, and began the story of his life. "I wasn't always like this," he whined, "but early in life I learned the motto I've lived by ever since: Sound mind; sound body . . . *Take your choice!*"

It's funny when articulated so clearly, but most of us did make such a choice early in life. Somehow we get the impression that athletes are stupid and programmers are flabby—and that we must choose one or the other. If you chose the flabby path in school, you were expected to spend all your spare time in the library, study hall, or computer center. If you were tempted to falter, you were buoyed up by colleagues who freely spoke of athletes in the most derogatory terms—when there were none present in the pub.

Previously, when I wrote about J. Gerald Simmons's "personal chemistry" for success, I emphasized the limits beyond which your body could not be pushed without affecting your brain. We could have diagrammed that relationship as in Figure 1. There we see that a good level of health increases work effectiveness and thus produces more slack time in which healthy practices can be pursued. This "diagram of immediate effects" can be analyzed (see, for example, our book, *On the Design of Stable Systems,* Wiley, 1979) according to the direction of influence of each box on the next. Through that analysis, we notice that the overall effect of traversing the loop is positive, so that, for instance, good health tends to produce better health.

This kind of "positive feedback" loop works either way, however. Poor health tends to produce poorer health. Why? By analyzing the loop we see that poor health diminishes work effectiveness (partly through diminished brain effectiveness), which in turn causes work to pile up, which in turn causes us to overwork, consume junk food in haste, and generally ignore our health. Finally, our health becomes even poorer, as the cycle continues spiraling—unless we can break it with a well-timed vacation or an understanding management.

But this kind of brain dysfunction is merely the grossest kind —akin to the effects of being struck on the braincase with a piano leg. The brain is not simply a beast of burden whose carrying capacity can be measured by a single number. The brain is a complex problem-solving device whose functioning we can only vaguely

Figure 1. The Positive Feedback Cycle of Health and Work Effectiveness

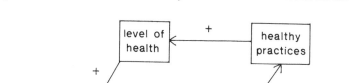

understand. We know the piano leg will put the brain out of commission, as will starvation, but that's like knowing the computer will stop if you pull the power cable or smash the CPU with a wrecking ball.

Some of the brain's diversity is suggested by elements on Simmons's personal chemistry list:

1. Articulate: Writing and speaking fluently in at least your native tongue.
2. Thoughtful: Weighing a question for a few seconds before responding.
3. Bright, informed, sparkling: "Difficult to define, but if a man or woman doesn't have it, it's immediately obvious—and that person comes over as dull."
4. Breadth of interest: Able to carry on an intelligent conversation without embarrassing gaps because of your lack of interest or education.

Simmons seems to suggest that you can somehow wipe a veneer of "chemistry" over your otherwise blah self. For instance: "brief reflection gives the impression that you have good judgment"—not good judgment, mind you, but the *impression* of good judgment. At this level of analysis, brain chemistry consists of a set of rules, such as, Count to three before you answer a question, so people will think you're thoughtful.

Oh, yes, a few rules like this can make you a better cocktail personality, or perhaps even land you a better job. You don't have to meet the same people at the next party, but if you land the job your brain will have to work at a deeper level. In real work, the veneer erodes all too quickly, revealing the lumps and hollows underneath. If you truly want to be more articulate, thoughtful, bright, informed, and sparkling, you're going to have to devote some time and effort to the job. And where will you find the time? My nonprogramming acquaintances tell me that programmers are the dullest people they know, but it's hard for me to believe them. Every time we start a new Becoming a Technical Leader Workshop, Sunday dinner is brighter and more sparkling than any Bohemian cocktail party I've ever attended. Only if you listen to the topics of conversation can you understand what the nonprogrammers are trying to tell us: From the noise and enthusiasm, you'd think programmers were talking about Etruscan marble or breeding the perfect rutabaga, but all they're talking about is *computers*—silly, dull, old computers.

We know that computers aren't silly or dull, and they're certainly not old. They're an endlessly fascinating subject, full of glorious detail, yet not lacking in opportunities for sweeping generalizations. But let's face it, there *is* more to life than computing. And, also, there are more parts to the brain than the parts we normally use in doing computing work. Not that we couldn't use those other parts to great advantage, if only they were kept fit by being exercised once in a while. Yes, and we'd do that, too, if only our heavy work load allowed it. But doesn't that sound familiar? Look at the loop of Figure 2, which has many similarities to Figure 1. Figure 2 is not addressing the physical health of the brain, but its spiritual health—not how *much* exercise it's getting, but *which qualities* are being exercised.

In our workshops we've repeatedly seen how stereotyped one's problem-solving behavior becomes when one works in a closed situation. Once we find one or two tricks that work well in our constrained environment, we tend to adopt those to the exclusion of all others. Most of the effectiveness of the workshop, I believe, comes from each participant's exposure to the problem-solving styles of other participants. On the job, though, the feedback loop of Figure 2 tends to dominate.

Problems in the computing business are getting more difficult with each passing month, so if we remain at the same level of problem-solving effectiveness, we soon accumulate a deadening backlog of work. With little slack time, we have little time for outside

Figure 2. The Positive Feedback Cycle of Mental Health and Work Effectiveness

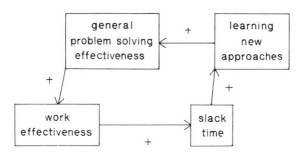

activities that stimulate those parts of our brain we don't ordinarily exercise at work. Therefore, our problem-solving effectiveness grows only to the extent that we are becoming a narrow specialist—which serves us poorly when we encounter new problems.

Brains require stimulation. If you're locked into a pattern of work, work, and more work, your brain soon habituates—the same way that it lets you stop hearing a clock ticking. So, if you want to be more effective at work, you must, paradoxically, be less single-minded in your devotion to work. Anything you do—*anything*—that stimulates new segments of your brain will make you a more effective programmer or analyst. I promise, with a money-back guarantee.

But notice that the brain must be stimulated. Not all the traditional mind-improving methods are stimulating. Quite the contrary. Many programmers and analysts, seeking this kind of stimulation, enroll in university courses. Although many of them are stimulated by these courses, many are not, for two reasons:

1. The course may be dull, yet they persist in carrying it through —perhaps because their employer is paying the tuition and they're embarrassed to quit in the middle.
2. The course may be too relevant to their work—that is, it may simply be more of the same diet they have on the job. That's not bad in itself, and it may provide useful facts, but it won't provide stimulation.

Generally speaking, you do better to get your stimulation outside of a formal educational system. Change your television-watching habits, for instance—not necessarily to something more intellectual, but just to something different from what you habitually watch. Or, if you never watch TV, it may prove a stimulating change, if only in a negative way. If you don't read anything except manuals, pick up any paperback on the way home tonight and read it. Stop, though, if it's dull. Or, if you do read, read something different, or stop reading for a few days and just open your eyes and ears and nose to the world around you. And, if you *must* take courses, take something your employer would *never* pay for. That way, you can quit if it's dull without fear of threatening your employment. And, even if it is dull, that may give you something in common to discuss with one of your classmates. Few of them will be computer people.

Why Don't I Run Out of Ideas?

I'm often asked, "Where do you get enough ideas for a column every week?" My usual answer is, "From readers like you"—and that's a major part of the truth. This essay, for instance, was triggered by a reader who sent in that very question.

Where *do* ideas originate? Fundamentally, there are only three sources of ideas:

1. Error
2. Theft
3. Copulation

The only truly new ideas come from mistakes. I get many from typographical errors. Once I typed "chance" for "change" and triggered a whole chapter in a book I was writing. Another time, I caught a client writing "turkey system" on the board instead of "turnkey system." This mistake gave me the opening I needed for a lecture on the perils of "off-the-shelf" systems (sometimes contrasted with "off-the-wall" systems).

But creative errors are rare. Or, rather, we rarely take advantage of our errors, probably because it's so much easier to steal new ideas. As a columnist, of course, I have thousands of readers, all working on good ideas for me. Once in a while, one of them reads a column and says, "Well, that's not bad, but my own thought on the subject is a million times better. I think I'll write that dull author and tell him what he really should be thinking." Not all these letters contain ideas as good as their authors think they are, but many do. So I have a steady supply of new material.

As a consultant, I get many of the same benefits, though I have to leave my typewriter to get them. Each client I visit is eager to tell me all the new ideas being put into practice in exchange for a similar set of ideas from me. After I've seen just a few clients, I've got more sensational ideas than I could use in a year of visiting other clients. Moreover, I don't feel the least bit guilty about "stealing" their ideas because I always give them their money's worth in return.

Naturally, I'm not talking about ideas my clients consider proprietary. I honor all my nondisclosure agreements with perfect obedience, and never reveal anything about which there might be the slightest doubt concerning my client's wishes. The ideas I steal are usually "trivial" ideas that the client takes for granted or doesn't even classify as "ideas" at all. They may be trivial in one shop, but when transplanted to the correct environment, they bloom into major breakthroughs.

Another factor in my favor is my ability to misunderstand something about the stolen idea, thus introducing an "error." As often as not, the error turns out to be the most creative and valuable part. Indeed, sometimes I feed the transformed idea right back to the originator, who now finds it worth a fortune. I recall one group of managers who told me they were planning to use their large computer to compile programs for some microcomputers they had purchased. I thought they said they were using the micros to compile programs for the big machine—at least to enter the programs and perform some operator assistance and error checking. When I mentioned that to another group in the same company, they went wild with enthusiasm and decided they too should have a micro for each programmer's personal use. Inasmuch as they were exceptionally poor typists, this approach freed them from the bottleneck the large machine was imposing on their development work.

But we eventually did even better. I learned that the micros were used to train data-entry clerks on simulated terminals. I naively asked why they didn't use the same software to train some of their programmers to be better typists. Their response was much screaming and yelling and tearing of hair, but I soon put an end to that because I don't have much hair to spare. Eventually, I tricked them into using the idea, with the result that some of their programmers got skilled enough at typing to make efficient use of the on-line facilities of the large machine. (*How* I tricked them is one of those trade secrets I'm not going to reveal just now.)

In the end, then, both stealing and blundering were excellent sources of ideas, but the greatest number of really good ideas has come from *copulation*—the coupling of two separate ideas to form a new and better idea than either one. You may like eggs, and you may like sugar—and you'll just *love* a good meringue.

The fundamental roles of error, theft, and copulation are magnificently illustrated in the genetics of living systems. Genetic systems provide the ideas on which each new generation is built. Sometimes a new idea is introduced through mutation (error), but most of the time the copying of chromosomes is done with great exactitude. That is, we steal most of our genetic material from our parents, but that's no crime because they stole most of theirs from their parents. Besides, like other ideas, genetic ideas aren't lost to their originators when they're stolen.

But unless you're unicellular (and sometimes even then), you got most of your endowment of original genetic ideas from recombining the material you stole from your parents. That's what makes you unique—just like everybody else. (Let's not hear from the identical twins.)

I need not go into details about how your mother and father happened to combine their genetic ideas to produce the wonderful person that is you. Suffice it to say that this combining process is regarded by many as the most pleasant part of the whole cycle. But, alas, not by everybody. Perhaps this explains why we often have trouble coming up with good ideas. When we're in school (at least when *I* was in school) we're taught an entire hierarchy of wicked things that we mustn't do, and these are often the very things that generate ideas.

When we turn in papers for grading, we discover that any mistakes are punished with bad grades. If we try to avoid mistakes by copying from the book, or from another student, we merely serve to escalate the scale of penalties. For a spelling or punctuation error, we may lose 10 percent of our grade, or even have to stay after school and write the correct answer on the blackboard a hundred times. But for copying, we're called "cheater" and sent down to the principal.

As for copulating, suffice it to say that if the school ever catches you, the punishment for cheating will seem like the Nobel Prize in comparison.

Now don't get me wrong. I'm not one of those lily-livered liberals who don't believe in the efficacy of punishment. Punishment is one of our most effective methods of teaching. It teaches you to avoid punishment. People who were repeatedly punished in school for error, theft, or copulation are unlikely to generate great ideas—out of fear of punishment.

As for me, I made my share of errors in school, and even cheated a bit now and then. Therefore, I still have some trepidation about making mistakes and remain, to this day, a bit squeamish about copying other people's work.

But, alas, I was a shy lad. I never managed the good fortune to be consoled in the bushes by Frieda, Valerie, Iris, Libby, or any of the other lovely young girls who shared my schools. Let alone get caught at it! Consequently, I never learned to fear putting two good ideas together to make one great one.

So here's my advice to any professional who lives and dies by great ideas: Live a clean, wholesome youth—or at least don't get caught and punished!

The Eager Beaver
and the Clever Cleaver: A Fable

It was a bad day for beavers, or so the beaver thought as the last tree he needed for his new dam fell the wrong way into the stream. He trimmed off the excess branches, but he knew he would never be able to move the stripped trunk from where it lay stuck in the mud. He must do something, but what was he to do, cut another one? This was the only tree big enough that was near the place it was needed, so even if he gnawed down another tree, he would still need help to drag it to the stream. To find help, he would have to run around to other beavers, and that would take until after dark. By tomorrow, he thought, there would be lots of water over the dam, and it might not rain again upstream for a month. He decided to run and find whatever help he could.

As he scurried through the woods, he suddenly felt something grab him by the throat, and he had to lurch backward to keep from being strangled. Rubbing his sore neck, he saw that it was the tent rope of some hikers who had moved into the neighborhood. "Just like people," he thought, starting to gather his composure to continue his mission.

Suddenly, a high-pitched voice from above his head said, "Watch where you're going! You almost sliced that rope in two, and if you did, this tent would fall down—and me with it."

The beaver looked up and saw a shiny metallic object suspended from the tent post. "Who are you?" he asked politely but impatiently.

"As you can plainly see," the object replied sharply, "I'm a cleaver. And who, pray tell, might you be, bustling about so busily that you almost wrecked our camp?"

"I'm a beaver, but I didn't recognize you, Mr. Cleaver. My eyes aren't that good, and besides, I don't believe I ever met a cleaver before. What do you do?"

"Oh, not much," the cleaver yawned. "Most of the time I just hang around here doing nothing. You see, I'm so keen that if I careened about the way you seem to be doing, everything around here would be cut to shreds. Why, take that tent rope, for instance. If I'd run against it as hard as you, it would have been cleft into two useless pieces. One can't simply muck about without being very, very cautious."

"On the contrary," the beaver replied, trying to end the conversation, "one can't just hang around all day doing nothing. There is work to be done all the time. If one didn't keep busy, busy, busy, nothing would be accomplished."

"Well, you can suit yourself," said the cleaver, cuttingly, "but then I'd appreciate it if you'd do your busyness elsewhere. I don't mean to be rude, for it's been nice talking with you, but I do have to continue my nap."

But the beaver wasn't insulted—indeed, he was only too happy for an excuse to resume his important affairs. Even so, he couldn't resist a parting comment: "You'll never cut the mustard if you don't stop hanging around that tent and start doing something." And, he thought to himself, idle hands are bound to make mischief. Why, look what he's done to me, that cleaver. I idled away so much time with him that I'll never find enough helpers to finish my dam.

With that he rushed back to the stream, for even though there was nothing he could do, he couldn't slow down. When he reached the stream bank, he was going so fast that he fell in, for the water was much higher than it had been before, and, of course, he couldn't see very well. When he swam to the surface, he looked around for the recalcitrant log, but it was no longer stuck in the mud. While he had been conversing with the cleaver, the rising water in the pond had lifted the trunk out of the ooze. The current was racing through the one open space, and had guided the log directly to its proper position in the dam. The work was finished, so there was nothing left for the beaver to do but enjoy a swim, since he was in the water anyway.

MORAL: Sharp teeth and sharp edges are fine tools, but they can be dangerous when used without thinking. Better to think and do nothing than not think and do damage.

IN OTHER WORDS: The ultimate in wisdom is knowing when to leave things to seek their own level and run their course.

Part V

Why Doesn't Everyone Understand Me?

Overrunning the
Output Recipient

During the first problem-solving session in our workshop, I witnessed a rare event. One of the students—very bright and very vocal—worked out an exact, clearly stated solution to the problem at hand. Given the circumstances of the class, such an exact solution is rarely found, and even more rarely communicated.

The solver—let's call him Mack—was working as part of a "division"—one half of the class competing with the other half of the class. He perceived how his solution could be applied, by coordinated action of the two divisions, "to achieve the maximum number of points." After some discussion, he convinced a few members of his division that he might possibly have the key to their problem. They indicated that if he could convince the other division to go along with his idea, they would follow.

What was rare about this event was not that Mack *thought* he had a complete solution—many students think that about each simulation. The unusual thing was that he actually *did* have a solution. Moreover, he could state his solution in precise mathematical terms. I winced as I watched him lay out his formula on the blackboard because he used APL notation. Some of the students understood APL, but others did not. Although they were all experienced programmers, and it would have been easy for Mack to explain his APL notation, he was so excited by his idea that he didn't notice that he had lost three-fourths of his audience.

As he continued, his audience raised other small questions about his idea, but he never really paused to answer them to everyone's satisfaction. Having constructed the problem, I naturally understood his solution, but I refused to give him or the others any sign concerning its correctness. In life, after all, there seldom is an omniscient judge sitting on the sidelines to say "hurrah" when you get the right answer.

Lacking a judge, Mack's solution had to stand or fall on his presentation. It fell. And with it fell Mack's credibility with the class, a credibility that he unsuccessfully struggled to recover for the rest of the week. The more he lost credibility, the harder he tried to present his good ideas on each exercise. The harder he tried, the faster he went; and the faster he went, the less people listened.

I wanted to tell Mack something that would help him restore himself to full acceptance by the class, but I was unable to conjure up an adequate image. After the class, however, a few of the students were sitting around exchanging war stories about the good old days. None of them had ever worked on a "naked" machine, without benefit of an operating system to handle I/O chores, so I tried to explain what fun it had been to program in that environment.

I was telling them about the PDP-1 I had used in the early 1960s to run psychological experiments. In order to write a magnetic tape that could be read on IBM equipment, I had to program each and every bit on each and every record going out of the machine. I had to write programs to compute the parity bit for each character, and the overall parity character for the entire record. That impressed them, but they were astounded when I explained that I also had to program the timing of each character's passage to the tape.

In other words, to keep the correct IBM spacing between characters, my program had to take precisely the number of cycles needed to move the tape that distance. Moreover, at the end of the record, it had to delay an additional small amount to give the correct spacing for the parity character. Then it had to allow for writing half of the interrecord gap. At the start of the record, the other half of the gap would be written, and timed, by my code.

"What would happen," one of them asked, "if your timing was off?" I explained that if the characters didn't get sent fast enough, the record would be too stretched out for the IBM equipment to read, but that wasn't the question that bothered him. "What I meant was, what would happen if you sent out the characters too fast for the tape?"

As I searched for an explanation, the image of Mack came into my head. "Well," I said, "it would be just like Mack on Sunday night, trying to explain his solution to the entire class. The characters would go out one on top of the other, producing gibberish on the tape, but there would be no indication to the program that anything was wrong. The only time you'd know that you'd overrun the output device was when you tried to recover the information on the record."

"Like Mack, when he couldn't understand why we didn't go along with his idea?"

"Precisely." I was sorry I couldn't have explained it as easily to Mack himself.

Mack, like so many computer programmers and analysts, had a very high I.Q. and knew many facts about computers and the rest of the world. He was fond of taking I.Q. tests, perhaps because it reassured him that he was a very talented person—in spite of the evidence he was getting from his colleagues, who never seemed to want to listen to him. Having a high I.Q. is like a CPU's having a terrific computing speed. It's a great asset in problem solving—as long as the problem doesn't involve a lot of input or output.

But when it's necessary to communicate with other people in order to convert the idea of a solution into an actual solution, that high internal speed commonly causes overrunning. Most of us have experienced being overrun at some times in our lives. Frequently, it was in school, where some professor believed the purpose of standing in front of the class was to demonstrate who in the room had the highest I.Q.

Another place we may be overrun is in books, especially if they are in subjects not quite in our own specialty. Albert Einstein once explained why this frequently happens:

Most books about science that are said to be written for the layman seek more to impress the reader ("Awe-inspiring!" "how far we have progressed!" etc.), than to explain to him clearly and lucidly the elementary aims and methods. After an intelligent layman has tried to read a couple of such books he becomes completely discouraged. His conclusion is: I am too feeble-minded and had better give up.

If the author of the book isn't an "authority," we may preserve our own egos by concluding that the author, not us, is feebleminded, as we so often do when reading manuals or computer science journals —and as we do when we listen to someone, like Mack, whose communication skills are several orders of magnitude below his raw intelligence.

If Mack were to encounter a computer system that was unbalanced in the direction of CPU power, he would instantly know precisely what to do to remedy the situation. He certainly wouldn't spend time trying to make the programs run even *faster*, but that's what he did when *he* was the system.

What Mack needed, and what so many bright young computer people need, is to build up their input and output capabilities until they are in better balance with their environment. When writing or talking, they can reduce the quantity of output and consume some of their excess computing power in improving the quality. I do not mean, however, sitting quietly between outbursts in a conversation polishing what you're going to say as soon as those other people shut up.

One way to trade computing power for improved output is to use a lot of that power processing the input. We usually call that "listening." It's sometimes hard to know when someone is listening —rather than merely waiting to seize control of the conversation. One way everyone knew Mack wasn't listening was by noticing how seldom he allowed other people to finish what they were saying. Why bother letting you finish, he seemed to be saying, when I know exactly what you're going to say and am prepared to go one or two steps faster?

It could be, of course, that Mack, as Einstein suggests, was merely trying to impress his classmates. If that was the case, he still failed, for few of them listened to him after the first couple of days.

They were about as impressed with him as I was with the PDP-1. It would have been great—if I hadn't known any better.

"If you want someone to like you," says an old Russian proverb, "let them do you a favor. If you want them to hate you, do them a favor." A similar wisdom applies to impressing people with your intelligence: If you want someone to think you're smart, listen and understand what they say. If you want them to think you're stupid, keep interrupting them with your great ideas.

Anyway, I thought you'd all like to interrupt what you were doing to hear these great ideas of mine.

RE-writing and the Preparation H Test

A number of people, some as authoritative as Edsger Dijkstra, have claimed that ability in native language—reading and writing—is the single most important asset a programmer can have. Although I don't believe that *anything* is the single most important asset a programmer can have, I do share their high opinion of the value of language ability.

Unfortunately, there aren't many publishers who think the same thing about programming authors. Perhaps good writers would be more attracted to the programming field if our textbooks seemed to place more importance on clarity. Perhaps more working programmers would concentrate on improving their own clarity if they had good role models among our authors.

Writing in English and writing in COBOL are similar activities, but not because COBOL is "like English." The secret key to all good writing is *re-writing*. It's true in English and it's true in COBOL. It's even true in APL. Nobody but a genius is capable of writing perfect prose on first draft. What a writer or a programmer needs is what Ernest Hemingway called "a built-in shit detector."

Let's see what Hemingway meant. Try reading the following paragraph. Then, if you like, try rewriting it using only half the words:

As we know all COBOL programs have four divisions. The first three—the identification, environment, and data divisions —specify various aspects of the program but do not describe any of the processing that is to take place. The actual instructions that specify what processing steps are to take place during the execution of the program are included in the procedure division. It is only through instructions in the procedure division that the programmer can communicate to the computer the operations that are to be performed.

Rewritten with no more than half the words:

Of the four divisions in a COBOL program, the first three— identification, environment, and data—do not describe any *processing*. The actual instructions specifying processing steps are found in the *procedure* division, and *only* in the procedure division.

I hope everyone agrees that the second one is worth the five minutes it took to construct it. Look at it this way: If a book is published containing the first example instead of the second, 12,000 readers are going to waste one minute apiece. That's 200 hours saved for a five-minute investment. And that's not counting any hours wasted by misunderstanding of a technical matter.

The key question is *How much time will be spent reading this material in the future?*

In the old days, we used to rewrite assembly language programs a dozen times to save three machine cycles. We usually don't have to do that now, because now the major cost is for people, not machines. Well, how many "people cycles" are we going to save by rewriting such things as the following "explanatory" comment:

```
THE FOREGOING DEVICE WAS NECESSARY IN ORDER TO
PERMIT THE SAME PROGRAMMING TO CALCULATE THE STA-
TIONARY AND THE STABLE POPULATIONS. ON THE FIRST
```

ROUND THE GIVEN VALUE OF R WAS ENTERED. ON THE
SECOND ROUND THE VALUE IN R WAS SAVED IN RR, R WAS
SET EQUAL TO ZERO, AND THE CONTROL TRANSFERRED TO
15. THE PROGRAM RECOGNIZED THAT IT WAS ON THE
SECOND ROUND BY FINDING ZERO IN R, AND IT THEN
TRANSFERRED TO 23, HAVING PUT THE STABLE POPULA-
TION IN THE ARRAY VKKA AND THE STATIONARY IN VKK,
FROM WHERE THE STATIONARY IS TRANSFERRED IN THE
LOOP AT 25 TO VLL.

I am sparing you the pain of trying to read the program this comment was attempting to explain. I'm sure you can imagine how much time a maintenance programmer will have to spend trying to understand it.

Don't fall into the trap of rewriting such comments. As long as the bull lives, there will be more such B.S. Comments as confused and confusing as this are not the disease: they are merely symptoms. If we cut open the code, we'd find a mess so repulsive we couldn't print it in a respectable publication. That's where the detector tells us to rewrite.

There are many symptoms signaling the need for rewriting a program, a comment, or a description. Most of them fall under the heading of "efficiency": If it takes more time to understand than it took to write, then rewrite or throw it away and start over.

Try this efficiency rule on the following gem:

In order to remove the time-consuming procedure of the program which initiated an I/O operation having to check periodically to see whether the operation has been completed or not, as well as to improve the overall performance efficiency of a computer, the interrupt facility was introduced.

You'll find—if you're typical of the readership of the manual from which this was taken—that you have to read this item several times to untangle its incredible subject. By the time you've done that, you've undoubtedly spent more time on it than the author did. In about the same amount of time, you can recast it into something that can be understood at one reading:

There are two principal reasons for a computer's having an

interrupt facility: (1) to eliminate the need for periodic program checking for termination of a parallel process, and (2) to improve overall performance efficiency.

Of course, when you rewrite so the sentence can be understood, you may find that it's not correct. In this case, we might not agree with this analysis of the principal reasons for the interrupt facility, or we might think that the second point is merely a repetition of the first.

Incorrectness is a symptom that surely signals the need for a rewrite. Sometimes the error is a direct result of poor writing, as in the following:

> However, like human memory, data can be placed in the computer's internal storage and then can be recalled at some time in the future.

The writer of this manual probably didn't intend to say that data were like human memory but, rather, that the computer's internal storage was like human memory. It probably would have been best to leave the mysteries of human memory to a physiology textbook, and rewrite simply as:

> The property that characterizes a computer's storage medium is the ability to accept data at one time and then to make that data available for recall at future times.

In programs, as in English text, indirectness or roundabout methods of expression usually indicate the need to rewrite. In programs we see such symptoms of indirectness as the following:

1. Introduction of superfluous temporary data elements
2. Loops with awkward exceptions or complex termination conditions
3. Moving and re-moving the same data items
4. Duplicated statements
5. Excessive housekeeping at start or finish

In natural English, we see similar signs, such as the excessive use of pronouns, repetitious prose, and difficulty of getting started or of finishing. In English, though, we have one particular syntactic structure that almost always indicates excessive indirectness—the passive voice. Several of the examples above could have been spotted as troublesome merely by observing their passivity. Sometimes, of course, the passivity is intentional, as in specifications or sales documents that don't want to commit the writer to anything.

We find many wonderful examples of passivity in advertising, particularly television advertising. The following example was supplied by Bob Finkenaur of Northeastern University. Preparation H is a popular American over-the-counter remedy favored by such professionals as programmers and analysts who spend much of their day exercising their posteriors. The most popular commercial for Preparation H states: "Preparation H is doctor-tested and helps to give prompt temporary relief from the discomfort of hemorrhoidal tissues."

To the sufferer, it sounds great, but on close analysis, we see that Preparation H

1. is *tested* by doctors, not necessarily approved
2. *helps,* but doesn't work alone
3. is *prompt,* but not immediate
4. works on the *discomfort,* not on the physical condition itself
5. gives *relief,* not cure
6. is *temporary,* not permanent

Next time you get a hardware or software proposal, try giving it the Preparation H Test. In fact, why don't we put all these tests together and call them the Preparation H Test? Whenever you read something intended for other eyes, ask yourself:

1. Is it more trouble to read than to rewrite?
2. Is it correct?
3. Is it misleading?
4. Does it give me a pain that only Preparation H can relieve?

If the answer to any one of these is yes, rewrite it. It may hurt the sales of Preparation H, but otherwise the world will love you for it.

Don't, however, apply the test to this work. Any problems here are *undoubtedly* due to poor editing or typographical errors.

Say What You Mean,
or Mean What You Say

"**T**hen you should say what you mean," the March Hare went on.

"I do," Alice hastily replied, "at least—at least I mean what I say—that's the same thing, you know."

"Not the same thing a bit!" said the Hatter. "Why, you might just as well say that 'I see what I eat' is the same thing as 'I eat what I see' !"

Alice was the prototypical programmer. So often, when reading code, I'm reminded of Alice's naive remarks at the Mad Hatter's tea party. Few programmers understand the difference between saying what they mean and meaning what they say. For instance, I once found this code in a PL/I program:

```
        I = 1 ;
XYZ:  A(I) = B(I) ;
        I = I + 1:
        IF I < 21 THEN GO TO XYZ ;
```

What does this code mean? Indeed, what does it mean to ask "What does this code mean?" One obvious meaning of a piece of code is the instructions it causes to be executed—its meaning to the computer. But far more important is the meaning to some other person who encounters this code for the first time and tries to understand it.

I'm particularly interested in the idea of how long it takes to understand a piece of code. This question is important for teaching, but much more important for the ever-expanding job of maintenance. In its lifetime, a piece of code is written once and read perhaps hundreds of times. Therefore, if it doesn't say what it means, and only what it means, it's going to add up to years of labor wasted in misunderstandings.

The above code was hard to understand for many reasons, most of which can be discussed under the query "Why wasn't it written some other way?" Alternatively, "If it meant something else, why didn't it say something else?"

For instance, the code seems to form a loop, with the variable I ranging from 1 to 20. But PL/I happens to contain a loop control structure, the DO, which was specifically designed for such loops, as in

```
DO I = 1 TO 20 ;
    A(I) = B(I) ;
END ;
```

If the programmer didn't choose to use this special form, the reader must ask, "Is there more to this than meets the eye?" Perhaps the label XYZ is used for some other purpose, such as a branch from outside the loop. That would justify this structure, for the language forbids us to branch into a DO. Or possibly there is some other reason, too subtle for us to perceive without help. But if, indeed, the programmer merely meant the same thing as the simpler DO-loop, she has said more than she meant and thereby given us a lot of grief.

Even the DO-loop may say more than it means. What's the special significance of the number 20? Does the programmer really mean

```
DO I = 1 TO N ;
    A(I) = B(I) ;
END ;
```

where N is the number of elements to be moved? In this form, the code says to move the elements of B numbered 1 through N to the corresponding elements of A, in order. That's pretty clear, but perhaps that, too, is more than was meant.

Possibly, what the programmer meant was

```
DO I = 1 TO HBOUND (A, 1) ;
    A(I) = B(I) ;
    END ;
```

which says move the number of elements in A from B to A, starting with element 1. In that case we don't have to search to discover what, if anything, was the special significance of 20, or of N. The program says less and means more.

But wait! What about the number 1? In PL/I, array subscripts don't have to start with 1, so perhaps the loop doesn't mean what we thought after all. It could be a trap for the unwary maintenance programmer, though it probably means "the number of elements in A." If that's what it was supposed to mean, then the programmer would have been kinder to write:

```
DO I = LBOUND (A, 1) TO HBOUND (A, 1) ;
    A(I) = B(I) ;
    END ;
```

which leaves no doubt in the reader's mind that we are moving the number of elements in the array A, regardless of what its bounds might be.

But there are still questions. This loop could have been written as

```
A = B ;
```

Why wasn't it? The reader has the right to ask, "If the program is simply moving one array into another, why didn't the writer use array assignment?" Must we assume that the writer didn't mean what she said? And if we assume that in one place, what stops us from assuming it everywhere?

Even the simple statement

```
A = B ;
```

leaves a lot of room for unintended meaning. If we're compiling the program for parallel processing, are we allowed to move all the elements at the same time? PL/I's definition says no, for there is a definite order in which the elements of B must be moved to the elements of A. We may not care about the order, but then again we may—if there are possible interrupts. PL/I doesn't really provide the language here to say what we mean, which might be

```
A = B, IN NO PARTICULAR ORDER ;
```

Also, it might seem that A and B are likely to be the same size, but that's not necessarily the case, considering only this statement. As long as B's bounds are contained within A's bounds, the assignment is permitted, so perhaps the programmer meant that in general B may be smaller than A. To find that out, we might have to look elsewhere, such as at the declarations of B and A.

In the original program, A and B were declared with the same dimensions, but in two separate statements that looked something like this:

```
DECLARE A(N) FIXED ;
DECLARE B (20) FIXED. . .
```

N was declared outside the procedure containing this code but was assigned the value of 20 just before the procedure was called. It all fit together, but if any one element was changed, it sprung a trap on the unwary maintenance programmer.

Indeed, there was good reason to believe that the value of N would change over time, in which case *at least* three places in the code would have to be changed to keep it current. Actually, A was a parameter array passed to the procedure, and its dimensions were set by the passed array. It could have been declared

```
DECLARE A(*) FIXED ;
```

But, then, what about B? When I studied the full declaration of B, I found it to be

```
DECLARE B(20) FIXED INITIAL ((20) 0);
```

which means it was to contain 20 zeros. Aha! It seems that B's only use was to set all the elements of A to zero upon entry to the procedure, which could have been expressed better by eliminating B altogether and writing

```
A = 0;
```

Expressed in this form, the code eliminates most of the other questions. It's not perfect, but see how much closer it comes to the ideal expressed by that greatest of all programmers, Humpty Dumpty: "When *I* use a word, it means just what I choose it to mean—neither more nor less."

If we only had more Humpty Dumpties, perhaps we'd have less rinky-dink programming.

Iatrogenic Pathology

$\mathbf{A}$lthough we imagine ourselves to be modern and free of superstitious nonsense, we do have some curious rituals. One of the most curious is based on the accident that most people have ten fingers. Over the years, this accident led our ancestors to develop a system of counting based on the number 10.

Because of this system, every tenth year ends in a zero, and the next-to-last digit changes. This change seems to catch some system designers by surprise, and several of my clients were caught short when 1979 turned into 1980. Many more, I suppose, will go down the tubes when 1999 turns to 2000, provided we haven't changed our number system by then.

I doubt that the number system will change. It's pretty familiar and we don't like the unfamiliar. Besides, most people—other than systems designers—have heard about the changing of the penultimate digit. Indeed, the common people actually anticipate the change with much excitement.

This magical significance of the number 10 carries over to the celebration of anniversaries of significant events in our lives, such as births, marriages, and graduations. And, because 10 happens to be divisible by 5, some of the magic seems to rub off on every fifth anniversary as well. For instance, graduations from high school and college are ritually observed on every anniversary ending in 5 or 0 by holding the "class reunion." Difficult as these rituals are to bear, most people don't have to endure more than one in any given year, because in the American system most people take four years to go through college after they graduate from high school. Although tradition sometimes seems nonsense, at times it serves a purpose that escapes our notice. In this case, the number 5 saves us from too many embarrassing comparisons with fellow alumni in any one year.

Alas for me, I took five years to complete college, so every five years I have to contend with two reunions. I'm not going to say which multiple of 5 this reunion represents, but this year my five-year debt has come due. I know I can't possibly survive actually attending these reunions, but I do feel I should do something to demonstrate my solidarity with the revered customs of our people.

I decided to spend fifteen minutes reflecting on what I learned in school—something unusual for a special reunion column. But I don't remember much about what I learned in school. It may be buried within me, or even woven within the very fibers of my being, but generally I can't extract specific items and say, "This I learned in school." With one exception! Much as I hate to admit this, there is one course I took that I remember clearly, the lessons of which I use every day, and which I consider myself most fortunate to have taken.

No, it wasn't my first computer course—I'm so ancient that they didn't even have computer courses when I went to school. No, not some fundamental math course. (Yes, you cynics, math had been invented a few years before my time.) Not some study of the immortal works of literature. Certainly not the one psychology course I ever took, for I dropped that after twenty minutes of the first lecture. No, the course I remember with such gratitude is nothing so grand as these, but a simple, unassuming course called "Scientific Greek." The course had been invented by a kindly old gentleman in the classics department as a way of preserving his job in a time when classics had reached bottom. Each week we were given a list of Greek roots that we had to memorize and regurgitate on a weekly examination. The words were spelled in English, so we didn't even have to learn the Greek alphabet.

It's a bit frightening to me, in view of my opinions about education, to recall how this course used nothing in the way of either analytical or creative ability. All that was required was memorization, pure and simple. The more you memorized, the higher your grade. True, the lessons on each root were surrounded by captivating anecdotes drawn from a lifetime of classical scholarship, but we didn't have to recall any anecdotes on the tests. True, the anecdotes might have helped us remember the roots, but though many of the roots remain in my mind to this day, I can't dredge up a single one of the stories.

The roots do come up all the time, and they're sometimes worth a fortune. More than once, in fact, they may have saved my life. Like the time I was laid out in a hospital bed with my neck swollen to size 40 from an infected tooth. An orderly wheeled in a cloth-covered cart. I heard metal instruments clinking under the cloth, so I managed to whisper, "What's that?" The attendant never even glanced in my direction, but automatically uttered these soothing words: "Oh, it's nothing. Just some stuff we need to do the tracheotomy."

As he wheeled and left the room, my scientific Greek bubbled up to my rescue. I'd never heard the word *tracheotomy* before, but I was immediately able to figure out from its Greek roots that they intended to cut my throat! Needless to say, forewarned was forearmed, and by the time the doctor arrived to do the dirty deed, I was ready to talk him out of it. And I did talk him out of it! I think he was caught off guard by my knowing what was about to happen. Routine medical procedure requires that the patient be kept in a state of ignorance until the last possible moment, and at that point the patient is asked to sign an "informed consent"—a document that gives the doctors several layers of legal protection against malpractice suits in case the surgery doesn't work out quite right. Or in case it's a success but the patient dies.

Because of my Greek, I had been able to prepare a number of questions to ask before I signed the consent form. Also because of my Greek, I was able to understand some of the answers to my questions, couched as they were in the otherwise secret language of medicine. Armed with these answers, I decided that I'd rather risk *not* having my throat cut for a little while, no matter how convenient it might have been for the doctor's schedule to do it immediately. Happily, the swelling started to respond to antibiotic treatment, and my throat remains intact to this day.

Recently, I was sick for several months with a mysterious ailment that no treatment seemed to abate. In desperation, my doctors put me in the hospital for tests and observation—a heartwarming place to spend the Christmas season. After five days of poking, probing, and prying, they seemed more baffled than ever. Two of them, charts in hand, had a mini-conference at the foot of my bed, and one said to the other, "Perhaps it's *iatrogenic.*"

"I was beginning to think that myself," the other agreed solemnly.

"Quite likely iatrogenic."

I believe the conversation was supposed to sound sufficiently ominous to induce me to submit to more severe treatment. But before the doctors could proceed, my scientific Greek flew once more to my rescue.

"Well," I said, "if you doctors are the cause, perhaps you ought to stop treating me altogether and let me go home." They seemed a bit startled that I had understood them, so I maintained my advantage and pressed for early discharge. Once out, I changed doctors and subscribed to a medical service that gets paid for *keeping* me well, not curing my illnesses. I've been feeling better ever since.

How nice, you're saying, but what does all this have to do with computing? Nothing directly, I suppose, because we programmers don't speak scientific Greek. But we do speak a kind of Pig Latin (JCL, front-end-database-microprocessor, distributed-intelligence-cyclic-network-architecture, COBOL-SNOBOL-SPITBOL, APLGOL-DAMMITOL) that serves many of the same purposes as the medicine man's Greek, Latin, and inscrutable handwriting.

And what purpose is that? Why, to conceal the *iatrogenic pathologies* from our pitiful corps of clients. Because just like the doctors, we need some way of concealing our mistakes other than covering them with soil and planting daisies. In medicine, *iatrogenic* means, literally, "born of the healing process"—in short, a disease caused by the doctors themselves. You've got to admit that *iatrogenic* sounds and smells a lot better. We've got to find a similar word for ourselves, but the Greeks didn't have any programmers, so what root could we use?

By the way, in case you're wondering why it took me five years to get through a four-year college program, I spent one year as the victim of an iatrogenic pathology. I didn't know it at the time—it was the year before I took the Greek course—but much later I figured it out. At the time, though, I not only didn't realize that the doctors had made me sick, but I actually thought they had saved my life! I was so impressed that I took up premedicine for a year before the truth dawned on me and I returned to computers.

And I'm glad I returned. In our business, who ever heard of a user who was so ignorant of both Greek and computing that he thought his tormentor was his savior? With our emphasis on clear communication, such an outrage could never occur!

How to Be Misunderstood
with Statistics

Once I've made up my mind, I love to hear arguments supporting my position. After I bought my diesel Rabbit, I began to collect articles extolling the virtues of diesels, Rabbits, and diesel Rabbits. After I lost a stone dieting, I consumed article after article extolling the virtues of slimness. And ever since I made up my mind that HIPO could safely be ignored, I've relished any and all evidence supporting the value of program listings and English narrative documentation.

Imagine my delight, then, when *Computerworld* of 21 May 1979 carried this provocative headline on page 33: DOCUMENTATION STUDY PROVES UTILITY OF PROGRAM LISTINGS.

As I devoured the article, I kept waiting for the "proof," savoring every paragraph. The article first explained the setting of the study: a research and development center for the U.S. Marine Corps that performs software maintenance on "all real-time, tactical computer programs in the corps." Then it listed the software documentation tools studied:

1. The Data Base Design Document (DBDD), which contains descriptions and pictorial representations of all program data structures

2. ANSI flowcharts (FLOW) as widely used [sic] in DP
3. Hierarchy diagrams (HIER), which show the calling hierarchy of a program similar to an organizational chart
4. Hierarchical-Input-Processing-Output charts (HIPO) as widely used [sic] in DP
5. Computer Program Listings (LIST), which at this installation provided interspersed source and object code, and also provided extensive cross-referencing and set/used information on all program elements.

Also on page 33, prominently displayed next to the headline, was the illustration shown here as Figure 3. I studied the diagram

Figure 3. How Various Documentation Types "Rate" with Programmers

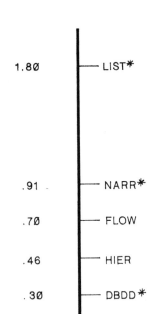

before turning to the continuation on page 37, hoping that perhaps here was the clue to the nature of the promised "proof." Then I noticed that HIPO had a "score" of 0.0 and an asterisk meaning "variation from average scores on starred items are significant beyond 0.90 level." I began to worry.

Why worry? First of all, I have a chronic difficulty with the statistical word "significant." To a statistician, "significant at a 0.90 level" means something like this:

"If we did this same study 100 times, and there really weren't any differences among the variables, we'd get as strong a result about 10 times."

To a reader, it means something further, by omission. The tradition is to cite levels of "significance" of 0.90, 0.95, 0.98, 0.99 and perhaps 0.999. It's also understandable that experimenters cite the strongest level their statisticians will permit. That means that if a 0.90 level is cited in the article, you can be sure that a 0.95 level wasn't reached.

There's nothing wrong, though, with this definition of "significant"—except that is has nothing to do with what nonstatisticians understand by that *other* word, "significant," which happens to be spelled with the same letters and pronounced in the same way. That one means, according to my dictionary: "Having a meaning; meaningful; full of meaning; important; notable."

You see, it *could* be "important" or "notable" that HIPO would get a score of 0.0 on a similar experiment no more than 10 times out of 100 if there weren't any differences among the variables. It could be, but there was nothing on page 33 to indicate that it was. Page 33, in fact, said nothing about where these numbers came from.

And that led me to worry about the 0.0. Now I happen to believe that the use of HIPO is not cost-justified in most of the places it's used, but I've never said its value was 0.0. Indeed, anyone who's worked with HIPO, or watched others work with it, would recognize that there is some value in the technique. The question I am asked as a consultant, however, is different: "Will the use of HIPO be worth what it will cost?"

To that question, I usually respond, "I don't know, but if you wish to experiment with HIPO, drop one other method first—one that puts a comparable cost burden on the programmers." When my clients do that, they sometimes find that HIPO is worthwhile. And sometimes they find that dropping the other method was even more worthwhile.

So the 0.0 was not very believable—until I noticed the word "normalized" in the figure. Now I understood. This figure is what we alternatively call a "Gee Whiz Graph." "Normalizing" the scores means scaling down the lowest to zero, which has the effect of maximizing the *appearance* of difference.

We don't know, and the article doesn't say, what the original scores were. They could have been 3.0 for HIPO and 4.8 for LIST. On the other hand, they could have been 497.1 for HIPO and 498.9 for LIST. It may not matter statistically, but it sure matters to the people trying to understand the significance (importance) of the graph.

Needless to say, I was discouraged, but deep devotion to my own opinions kept me going long enough to turn to page 37 for the conclusion of the article. There I discovered that these numbers were not the outcome of some experiment with documentation tools, but the "results of a questionnaire" given to eighteen programmers. An opinion poll!

These results, according to the authors, "show that LIST is clearly *regarded* as the superior tool" (my italics).

Regarded? My dictionary gives these three definitions of *regard* (among others):

1. To observe closely.
2. To look upon or consider in a particular way.
3. To have great affection or admiration for.

In short, though the headline writer inferred the first meaning of *regard,* the second or, even more, the third seems a more appropriate choice in this case. What this study "proves," it seems to me, is that it's quite likely that these eighteen programmers have more affection for LIST than they have for HIPO.

I want to be fair to the authors of the study and warn you that an essay may not provide the whole story. I'd guess, though, that it's pretty close to the essence. And the essence is this: we're now to choose software tools the same way we choose cigarettes or deodorants.

I can see it now. "Nine out of ten chief programmers prefer subroutines." "I've been a Fortran user ever since I started programming, and I'd rather fight than switch." "Be a *real* programmer—don't use virtual machines!"

Come to think of it, isn't that what we've always done? Yes, but now we have statistics and experimental psychology to support our prejudices. Who says software engineering has no future?

A Lesson from the University

$\mathbf{M}$y oldest son Chris has been attending classes at various universities for about ten years. At first he would cut his high school classes and visit the university to attend lectures on subjects he found interesting. Later, he dropped out of high school altogether and just started attending university courses without registering.

After a few years, Chris earned a high school diploma by examination and began his attempt to be a regular college student. Somehow the regularity of this position didn't fit well with Chris. Each semester, he would register for five courses and drop three of them. Sometimes he didn't bother to drop, but just flunked by not attending class. Finally, he realized that he was wasting a lot of money this way and that he had no future in the university as long as he was a regular student.

Chris has always been interested in horticulture. He accepted a position on the university grounds staff that allowed him to work outdoors, earn a little money, and even take a course or two at university expense. This new arrangement seems to suit him. He's got a nice suntan, good strong muscles, and almost every day he learns something. As far as I can tell, though, most of his learning comes on his job, not from his two courses.

The other day Chris began complaining about his boss, who has been on the grounds crew more than forty years and is getting very close to retirement. I asked Chris if his boss was such a good worker that they wanted to keep him on past retirement age. "No," he said, "he hardly works at all." Well, he must be a very good supervisor. "No," Chris said, "we do pretty much what we want—he's hardly ever watching us or even to be found when we're working." Well, does he have some kind of blackmail information over the university administration, so they're afraid to let him off the job? "No, that's not it either," said Chris, "although that's perhaps a little closer to the truth. The fact is, he's the only one who's been around so long that he knows where all the underground pipes are buried. He may not do anything for several months, then one day they're about to dig up some new area of the campus so they'll come to him and ask him to locate the buried pipes. He remembers them all, and this can save the university thousands of dollars in mistakes like cutting into a water pipe when they're digging a trench. I'm sure he earns his salary many times over just because of the information that he has in his head."

Naturally, I was unable to let this lesson pass without drawing a moral. I pointed out to Chris that this was the Way of the World. You're paid more for what you know than for what you do. Chris could break his back a thousand times and never have the job security his boss has just from knowing where all the pipes are buried.

The situation is no different in computing. Unfortunately, management in many computing organizations doesn't seem aware that most of the important documentation is being carried around in people's heads. Managers get very upset at the idea of paying someone whose only function is remembering how things were or why they are the way they are. Management wants to pay for lines of code or some other tangible sign of effort.

The conceptual problem that data-processing managers have with this type of worker stems from their confusion between documentation and documents. In this respect, there's a very strict parallel between landscaping and programming. In landscaping, the basic documentation is in the ground. If your map says there's no pipe in a certain place and your shovel hits a pipe, you have to

believe the shovel. The same is true if the map disagrees with old Fred's memory. Fred is more likely to be right than the map. But the shovel is the final judge.

In programming, the code is the ground. There may be lots of other paper documents lying about, but what they're lying about most of the time is the code. Every good maintenance programmer knows this and, indeed, rarely looks at the documents that are supposed to document the system under maintenance. When a question arises that can't be answered directly out of the maintenance programmer's own head, the first source of information is old George who worked on this system a couple of years ago. Nine times out of ten, George can give the information you need.

The other one time out of ten, George is likely to be able to answer, "Who else might know?" Perhaps he refers you to Sally, and Sally has nine chances out of ten of knowing the answer. Once in a while, George or Sally will refer you to some document, but that document is likely to have been superseded by some other document, which is more up-to-date but doesn't happen to have the information you want.

The previous description was not intended as an editorial comment, simply a description. Programming managers would do very well to study that description and then compare it with the process that actually takes place in their own organizations. Management is a difficult business. It's made more difficult by managers who are afraid to start from the base of reality in thinking about what to do in their organization. If you would like to improve the documentation situation where you work, wouldn't it be a good idea to start with a clear picture of what that situation is right now?

The next step in a program of improved documentation is to see what can be done to assist the natural processes of documentation before trying to introduce artificial methods. For instance, since the code is the basic ground upon which all documentation is based, why not take steps to improve the quality of the code as documentation? The first step in such a code-improvement program is to be sure that no code goes in the library without having been read and understood by one or more people. If the code is a document, it stands to reason that it can only be tested for its documentation power by being read. Once your organization starts reading code on a regular basis, many other ideas will spring to life about how to improve the code's readability.

While you're improving the code as document, you might also look around to see what can be done to improve the quality of *individuals* as documents. As a first step, you should notice that when individuals leave an organization, they lose most of their usefulness, just as documents do. Therefore, any policies that reduce employee turnover are likely to improve the quality of the living documentation.

To some extent, you might protect yourself from turnover by capturing some of this living documentation on a recording. Audiotape is fine, but videotape is even better. Why not have the designers on each part of the system take a few minutes in your company's video studio to record the thought process that went into the design —the thought process that will be lost to view after a few months? In a short time, you'll accumulate a nice library of video documents, which at the very least can be used to introduce new people to your projects. They'll not only see the thinking that went into the project, but they'll also be introduced to the personalities who are the living documents they will refer to when necessary.

If you don't have videotape, or even if you do, you might want to create other forms of indexing that will guide people with questions to people with answers. For instance, each piece of code might contain a prologue that cumulatively lists all the people who ever laid a hand on the code. Another method that's often used is to have each line of code contain the initials of the last person who worked on it. That way, if the maintenance programmer is having some difficulty with a particular line, there's no trouble locating the person who has the most recent direct knowledge.

Even your regular paper documents should contain an adaptive index to the people who worked on or used them. At the university, there are maps of the grounds dating back seventy years. These maps are useless without the learned commentary of one of the old-timers who remembers, for instance, that there was an error in this map when they used it in 1937. And sure enough, they never did correct the error even though they did the right thing underground. Indeed, the more imposing the document scheme, the less likely it is to be updated by the ordinary mortals who have to use it. No groundskeeper is going to place dirty, ugly handwriting on the beautiful drawing made by the architect in 1910.

In the same way, no programmer is going to despoil the documents left by the designers of our holy system. But any programmer who tries to use the documents will remember very vividly how long it took to understand a certain paragraph. That programmer will be more than happy to help the poor novice who's now trying to understand that paragraph. If you provide a place on each document for people to initial when they've read a document and understood it, later readers will have a reference to those people who are most likely to be of assistance.

I could give many more examples of how you could enhance your own living documentation system, but it's better if you know and study your own system and develop your own suggestions. Only then will my suggestions be completely relevant to your own problems. I've gotten any ideas I have on the subject from organizations who have done just that—studied their own informal documentation system and looked for ways to help it along.

So let that be a lesson to all of you who say that the university never teaches anything. The university teaches many things. If you recall your own university years—assuming you went to one—and if you're honest with yourself, you'll realize that you, too, learned many things at the university. Possibly, you didn't know that, because you were concentrating on the learning that took place in the formal part of the university—just as you concentrate on the formal part of your documentation schemes. Most of the learning at the university takes place outside the classroom, just as most of the documentation in the programming shop takes place outside the formal system of documents.

The Mouse and the Iron:
A Fable

One Tuesday, a mouse was exploring the kitchen when he happened to get on top of the ironing board. On the board was an electric iron whose face was so shiny he could see his reflection in it. As the iron was tilted a bit backward, his reflection seemed to him to be another mouse who was a bit shorter than himself. As he was a lonely mouse, he took the size of the reflection to mean that this new mouse was a girl.

Shyly, he moved a bit closer to the stranger. With equal shyness, she advanced toward him. Cautiously, he smiled; and just as cautiously, she smiled back. As can be imagined with such a responsive partner, he quickly fell head over heels in love.

They sat for a while, gazing into each other's eyes in loving rapture, until the lady of the house opened the kitchen door. "Run," he commanded his sweetheart, and they scampered away from the iron. Glancing back for a moment, he saw that she was indeed running away, but in the other direction. "She must live over in that neighborhood," he thought.

All the next week he looked for her on the opposite side of the kitchen, but she was nowhere to be found. On Tuesday, however, the ironing board was set up again and the iron was put on top and plugged in. As soon as the lady of the house had left the room, he scooted up on the board. Sure enough, there in the iron was his true love. As he ran up to her, he could not conceal his emotions; and he saw that she could not conceal hers either. He reached out to her, and she reached out to him. They touched paws. They kissed. He was overcome with emotion, though enough in control of his senses to see that she was likewise overcome. He kissed her again, and it seemed to him that her kiss was growing warmer.

Again and again he kissed her. Now her growing warmth was unmistakable. Indeed, he was becoming so warm that he had to move away from her a bit to cool off. He smiled and told her things about himself. Though she did not answer (he liked women who were good listeners), he felt by her smiles that she was responding to what he said. At last, he could resist her charms no longer, and he rushed forward to kiss her once again.

By this time, of course, the iron had reached its full heat. "Eeeow!" he cried, jumping back with burned mouth and paws. "Why did you do *that?*" But before she could reply, the lady of the house came in, so they both had to run away.

All week he brooded about what he had done to offend his friend. Perhaps he had been too forward. Or, perhaps, not forward enough. On the other hand, he *had* spent a lot of time talking about himself. Perhaps that is what she found offensive. "Next time," he resolved, "I will let her tell me about herself. I will beg for forgiveness."

On Tuesday next the ironing board came out again. He rushed to see his love, and his heart was pounding for fear she would not come. But she was there, and as the iron was not plugged in, she received him in a friendly, though somewhat cool, manner. They passed a pleasant hour, kissing and holding paws, and not a word was said about their previous trouble. Before he had a chance to bring it up, the kitchen door was opened, and they had to part for another week.

For the mouse, it proved another week of brooding. Delighted as he was that she had taken him back, he could still recall the coolness which she had not shown before. He finally decided that he must be very careful on their next meeting.

That meeting was delayed for more than an hour, because the lady of the house stayed in the kitchen while the iron was warming and did not leave until the ironing was finished and the iron unplugged. No sooner was she out of the room than the mouse leapt up on the ironing board and raced into the outstretched arms of his darling. "Eeeow!" he screamed as he ran right into the searing iron. "Why did you do *that*?"

He questioned her, pleaded with her, even confessed to her all of his shortcomings; but she would not tell him what he had done wrong. At last, however, he began to detect a change in her attitude, even though she had not said anything. "Perhaps," he wondered, "she has forgiven me, seeing that I have been punished enough." He moved forward to her and, sure enough, she returned his kiss and embrace, with all the warmth of their second meeting.

And so it went from Tuesday to Tuesday, sometimes hot and sometimes cold. The poor mouse was soon covered with scars from the branding of the iron. Worse than that, he became so preoccupied with trying to understand his girlfriend's behavior that he started missing meals and losing weight. Finally, one Tuesday, right after seeing her, he was so distracted and hungry that he blundered into a mousetrap, which ended the misery of his ill-starred love.

MORAL: If you are foolish enough to suppose that the iron turns hot and cold for you, you are foolish enough to get burned.

IN OTHER WORDS: Communication always involves two people, not one plus iron.

Part VI

How Can I Survive in a Bureaucracy?

Job Rotation
Around the Mid-City Triangle

You've heard of the Eternal Triangle—the perpetual intertwining of human libidos and marital arrangements. You've heard of the Bermuda Triangle—the unending mystery of ghost ships and ghoulish sailors. But until now, only I have known of the curious circulation of programmers among the Big Three of Mid-City, U.S.A.

I was visiting Mid-City for the third or fourth time when I became aware of a peculiarity shared by many of the programmers I had met on previous visits. Mid-City has three principal data processing installations: Amalgamated Egg Sucking, Central Cane Testing, and United Cigar Rental. Among them, they employ 70 or 80 percent of the programmers in Mid-City, perhaps 600 in all. Of the programmers I met, those with ten or more years' experience seemed to have worked at all three installations. Some, indeed, were on their second time around what I came to call the Mid-City Triangle.

In a larger city, I would never have noticed the phenomenon because in a larger city the programmers' choices are too varied. In a smaller town, it always seems to be work at Big Daddy's or move out. In Mid-City, though, the cycle was pure and perfect.

It went something like this: Brent Bleary graduated from college and joined the new employee training program of Amalgamated, though it could equally well have been one of the others. Having completed his six-month COBOL course, he was given a small application program to write. He was challenged and he was happy. All day long he coded, submitted jobs, pored over bugs, and wove in changes. Finally, only a few weeks after the scheduled date, he delivered his masterpiece, and the boss was mightily pleased.

Brent was rewarded with an even more challenging new application, and he set to work whistling to himself with joy. But a few weeks into the new project, he was interrupted by a minor annoyance—someone wanted a small change in his first program. But Brent took it in stride, even though his documentation had gone cold on him, and soon he was back to application two. In the following months, these little interruptions came more or less regularly, but they never amounted to more than an irritating diversion from his main task of the moment.

When application two was delivered only a week late, Brent was praised a thousand times and raised a thousand dollars. He even rewarded himself by taking a short vacation in a cabin on a nearby lake. Unhappily, his vacation was cut short when an old geezer brought him an urgent telegram from town: One of his applications had crashed!

Yet even then, if Brent had regrets about his abbreviated vacation, they were drowned in the importance he felt at being the center of attention while the problem was being fixed. And when he was given application three—the very job he had been hoping for—all thoughts of vacation—past, present, and future—dissolved.

The work on application three went well—at least when Brent wasn't being interrupted by little fixes and enhancements and questions and clarifications and hand-holding on applications one and two. When his manager inquired about the schedule of application three, Brent answered with a query of his own. When was he going to be relieved of some of this pesky maintenance work so he could concentrate on the important job at hand? It wouldn't be long, he was reassured. Just as soon as one of the new trainees completed the COBOL course.

But the course ended and no trainee was forthcoming. There were urgent jobs to be handled and not enough time to have Brent turn application one or two over to someone inexperienced. Indeed, it would take Brent less time just to handle the few requests himself than it would to teach some trainee all that he knew about the subtleties of the applications. Brent had to agree with that argument, for he was certainly too busy with application three and his maintenance chores to find time to train some greenhorn.

And so another year passed, and Brent was now the proud father of quintuplets—applications one, two, three, four, and five. He had an application six on the way, but its gestation period was getting longer and longer, since Brent had less than a few good hours a week to work on it. His manager had promised relief from the maintenance several times. Once it had been very close, but then his manager got promoted and the new manager just couldn't afford any risks until things had settled down.

Then, one evening, at the meeting of the local chapter of the Society for Computers and People, Brent heard that Central Cane was desperate for some experienced programmers to work on an exciting new development project. He made a few inquiries, arranged an interview, and took his Programmer Aptitude Test. He was offered a job, at a moderate increase in pay, but with the greatest fringe benefit of all. If he worked at Central Cane, he wouldn't have to maintain any of the Amalgamated programs any more. All he would have to do is develop a wonderful *new* program. It was like replacing the old jalopy with a brand new sports car—at reduced monthly payments!

But if Brent was anything, he was loyal, so he gave his manager one last chance. And, indeed, the manager was overflowing with sympathy for Brent's plight, welling with confidence that relief was coming in a few months, and brimming with news of the fat raise he had just negotiated to keep Brent happy in the interim. Brent thanked his manager for the raise, quietly left his office, and immediately called the personnel manager at Central Cane to accept the offer. When his manager found out, he was completely befuddled. How could someone quit just when he got such a nice raise and such warm sympathy?

Well, to make a long story short, Brent's stay at Central Cane pretty much followed the same script as it had at Amalgamated. After a glorious honeymoon with his virgin application, he was soon saddled with an ever-fatter, nagging burden of maintenance of his previous triumphs. Eventually, he heard that United Cigar was getting into new territory, and after a few formalities he found himself across town in a freshly painted office, freed forever of the oppressive programs and management at Central Cane.

But after two years, when the cycle had completed another turn, Brent had run out of places to go in Mid-City. In Gotham City, he might have kept on going to new firms forever, but here— what was he to do? As the months wore on, he began to despair, even considering a career in some new area, like calf-roping. Then, by chance, he ran across his old manager from Amalgamated.

Brent was worried that there might be some residual bitterness, but in almost five years all had been forgotten and forgiven. Besides, Amalgamated was currently in the process of automating several large new applications, so the manager wasn't in any position to offend anyone who had programming experience. In a short time, Brent had packed up his templates and his job-control decks and shipped them back to Amalgamated. Not to his old desk, though, for now he was a very senior programmer and had a semiprivate office to hang out in. But more important, nobody even remembered that he had had anything to do with applications one through six all those years ago. Or at least they were too polite to mention it.

I stayed a few extra days in Mid-City, just to interview some of Brent's contemporaries, like Sue, Harry, Betty Anne, Irma, Wolfgang, and Thelma. With minor variations, all had the same story to tell. Wolfgang, in fact, had been around the Mid-City Triangle twice and was in the process of negotiating his third circuit. Where would it all end? I wondered on the plane back. What would it take to break the grip this iron triangle had on so many lives? Or was it these people who had the grip on the triangle? As I recalled each interview, I realized that these were all happy programmers, perhaps far happier than the average. I wondered who's getting stuck with all that maintenance?

(I'd like to say more about this essential subject, but I have so much to say I'm saving it for another book. If you can't wait, I suggest you look at Girish Parikh's book *Techniques of Program and System Maintenance* to find out what some people are doing to escape the dreaded Mid-City Triangle syndrome.)

Large Organizations, Small Computers, and Independent Programmers

I've always allowed my life to be influenced by a few great books—the Bible, *The Interpretation of Dreams*, Gandhi's autobiography, *Alice's Adventures*, and *The Hunting of the Snark*. Among the many things the Snark taught me was that anything I hear three times must be true. Using that insight, I can sit at my desk in the Breadbasket of America and take the pulse of the entire nation, even the world.

Here's how it is done. If in any one week I get three letters and/or telephone calls on the same trend, then I know it's really happening. In this way, I can know when skirts are going up or stocks are going down. I don't have to read newspapers or watch the tube, for they're always days or weeks late in sensing the news.

Recently, I spotted a new trend that I'm going to share with my readers. My first clue came in a letter on Monday from Claude, a former student now programming for a large food company in Indianapolis. Toward the end of the letter he wrote, "My wife and I recently bought a Radio Shack computer and we're having a marvelous time. She's a retired programmer, so when the kids aren't around she spends all her time developing nifty software. The minute I get home from work, she goes into the kitchen and I take over the machine. And once the kids are in bed, we work together. We've already developed three small packages which we're selling locally, and hope to get into national distribution. When you're in town, you'll have to come over and take a look at our product line. If these sell well, I might retire from the company. As it is, I spend most of my day in the office working out routines to try at night when I get home. Nobody's the wiser—they never could keep me busy here."

That very afternoon I received a call from an old friend in southern California. Joanna has been programming for a large manufacturer for about sixteen years, and we were arranging a consulting visit to her firm. "And when you're here," she said, "you'll have to go computer shopping with me. I've decided to buy a home computer, but I'm taking my time so I get the right system."

Being conservative by nature, I asked, "Are you sure you'll be able to tolerate such a small machine after having been spoiled by the facilities of the big ones?"

"Not to worry. I've worked on machines my friends have, and I've discovered that whatever I lack in tools and capacity, I can make up because of the complete control I have over the situation. It's more or less the same setup I worked with when I started, back when I got hooked into this business in the first place."

"Life *was* simpler, back then . . ."

"My only worry is that when I can satisfy my addiction without going to the office, what do I need Big Daddy for? If I can get my fix at home, I might never leave. But I don't care. What fun it will be!"

But two communications don't make a trend, particularly if one of them is from a junkie in southern California, home of oranges and nuts. It wasn't until Thursday that I got my next call—from David in Washington.

David was one of our prize pupils of all time. He went to one of my earliest workshops and immortalized himself in our hearts and minds. Every few years, when I'm in the nation's capital, I pay him a visit, but this was the first time he'd ever called. By now he'd advanced himself from programmer to manager of systems development, and I'd always imagined him to be a person too busy for idle phone calls. Apparently, though, he just wanted to exchange gossip and news.

News from the office was resoundingly dull, but David's voice became animated when he started to talk about his new venture. "In the evenings, as early as I can slip out of the office, I'm doing systems analysis on a consulting basis with five or six small businesses here in town. I work out the specifications for what they need, then I turn them over to a service bureau that has two minis and is getting a third."

"I'd think you'd be tired of that kind of work at the end of a full workday," I offered.

"Just the opposite. I almost *never* get to do any analysis work at the office anymore. And when I do have a good idea, it takes so long and so much aggravation to get it implemented, it sucks all the joy out of it. With the little businesses, I get to work on the whole problems, they listen to me, and I start seeing results sometimes in a few days. It's really gratifying—just like the old days."

"What does the office think of this activity?"

"Oh, they don't know about it. In fact, you're the only one I feel I can talk to about it. I suppose I'd get in trouble if they discovered I was moonlighting, at my salary. But I'm not doing it for the money—my regular job takes good care of that. Consulting gives me something I just can't get any more at work. I really feel alive again."

"Any chance that you'll quit and go into it full time?"

"I don't think so, though the service bureau keeps begging me to send them more work. They've got lots of potential customers, but can't get good systems work except from me and a few others in the same situation. But I don't think it's worth the risk. Why should I? I've got a lifetime job here, at good pay, and they don't make many demands. I suppose if they found out and made a fuss, I'd have to lay off the consulting, but it's not likely to happen. In any case, they wouldn't fire me. They never fire *anybody,* and my work is still twice as good as they expect."

David hadn't been off the phone long enough for me to reflect on his situation when another call came in, this one from Sawyer, who works for a computer company in Silicon Valley. Sawyer was a student of mine way back in my university days and now has become quite a mature programmer. He worked for three different manufacturers since he left school, before landing his present job about two years ago.

As it turned out, Sawyer was seeking some information on how to form a corporation with two of his friends. "We're doing contract programming," Sawyer explained, "and we're making so much money that we thought we'd better become more like a real business."

"I thought you had a regular job."

"Yes, but they've given me a terminal so I can work at home, and I can do all their work in less than an hour a day. The rest of the time—when we're not riding our bikes—I work on improvements to packaged software for minis that local businesses have bought."

"Are you selling packages?"

"No, we just customize them. None of the manufacturers pay any attention to these people after they've paid for the iron, so we go in and for fifty dollars per hour, we fix them up any way they want them."

"You'll never get rich that way. The manufacturers have the right idea. Mass-produce, make the sale, then disappear. That's where all the profit is."

"Well, we don't really want to get rich, but we're doing all right. For one thing, we all have regular jobs to give us a nice base. And the customers love us. They'll pay whatever we ask, because they've been abandoned by the manufacturers and don't know where else to turn. Besides, we're beginning to develop little things we can sell to more than one place. We charge each one just what it would cost to develop it new for them, even though we might only have to make a few adjustments to something we did somewhere else."

"Sounds good," I said, "if you can keep getting away with it."

"No sweat. They're so desperate for programmers out here that they'll never question what I'm doing. Hey, would you like to go into business with us?"

And you know, I was sorely tempted. I think I would have accepted the offer, if only I had a regular job to pay my salary and benefits while I was becoming an independent capitalist. Come to think of it, why am I sitting here slaving over a typewriter? The starving writer in the garret is out of fashion in this era of cheap hardware and costly people. If I *really* want independence, my first step is to answer one of those tempting ads—you know, the kind that devote most of the space to telling you about vacations, employee benefits, and recreational opportunities in the area. Then I can get settled into my office, get my manuals and my terminal, tack up my cartoons, and start planning when I can work on my new business without being spotted. Let's see, where did I put those ads?

Management Views
the World by Moonlight

Some time ago, I published the previous essay about the trend toward moonlighting on small computers by professional programmers. The essay told the stories of Claude, Joanna, David, and Sawyer—pseudonyms for real friends of mine who had taken up moonlighting for a variety of reasons. I wasn't terribly concerned about getting any particular person in trouble because the essay was published in England. But when I decided to publish it more widely, I sent a copy to Claude, Joanna, David, and Sawyer to make sure I had sufficiently concealed their identities. They were amused; they were flattered. But they also were a bit anxious. As Claude put it, "Do you want to blow the whistle on us?"

I doubted that I would be blowing the whistle, for I was sure that this widespread phenomenon couldn't escape notice for long. Perhaps management already knew about it. I decided to take a poll among firms similar to those employing Claude, Joanna, David, and Sawyer. I wanted to know if the managers knew. And if they knew, I wanted to know what they did about it.

There were two kinds of reactions. One was outrage and fear, expressed by one manager in these words: "You shouldn't publish this. I have a nasty feeling this parable may be taken literally."

I more or less expected this fearful reaction, but the other type of response frankly surprised me. In the words of one manager in another division of Claude's company, "I've been aware of this kind of activity among our programmers for three years. Naturally we can't make a public acknowledgment, but our policy is very simple. As long as their names aren't used in public, and as long as their work here gets done, we don't mind at all. In fact, in my perception, people around here are a lot happier since this sort of activity began. We're big. We're bureaucratic. There's no way we can enrich these jobs enough to satisfy the top 10 percent of our people.

"But if our top people get bored, we lose them. We need them for their expertise, but not all day every day. So we turn our heads and don't notice what they're doing. If I were ever challenged by upper management, I'd argue that the time the employees spend in our office working on such things is training. And more effective and efficient training than we can devise. One of my new managers was promoted after two years of working with an outside bureau. During that period, I watched him grow in several personal dimensions. There was nothing in his job assignment here that could have given him that kind of experience. I'm sure it was his outside work that did it."

A third manager explained how he had accidentally started this kind of practice in his rather staid and traditional financial firm. "My racquetball partner asked me for some advice about getting a computer for his auto parts business. I told him that he needed someone good who could act as a consultant over a long period of time. I warned him about all the inexperienced, unreliable kids who were getting into this business, but I couldn't come up with any suggestions about how he could do better. That same afternoon, my most senior programmer was waiting to see me. He was threatening to take a more lucrative offer, but there was no way with our policies that I could match it. He would have been making more than me! He was actually worth it, but our company just would never accept a technical person earning more than his manager.

"I offered him a promotion into management, something he'd turned down many times before. It just wasn't his bag, and I admired him for being able to say no. As he walked out of my office, for some reason I flashed on my racquetball conversation. I phoned my friend and asked him what he'd pay for one of my best people to put in a few hours a week as a consultant. It was more than enough to match the difference between what I could offer and what my programmer had been offered at the other job. I called the programmer back into my office and rather tentatively asked him if he'd consider such an arrangement. He was delighted. He really likes his job here, and he wasn't looking forward to moving out of town for the new job. So I kept my best technical person and made a friend happy at the same time. Of course, now that other people in the office are doing the same thing, I can hardly object. But it does make me watch them more carefully to see that they are getting the job done here, rather than just putting in the time. And I do wish our firm would accept the fact that a technical person could fall outside the usual salary scales, but I doubt that will ever happen. So we'll probably keep using this dodge for the duration."

Another manager told me how he personally had moved from outrage to acceptance. "When I discovered the first such case in our shop, I wanted to walk right out to the guy's desk to fire him on the spot. I must have been red with rage, but fortunately it was after office hours. I had the whole night to cool off, and I didn't do much sleeping. By morning, I realized that I was taking the whole thing personally, as a challenge to my authority. I decided to hold off for a few days. Then I discussed the matter with my boss, as a hypothetical case. She put me on the right track with a single question: 'What is this telling you about the environment you've created in your department?' I was stunned, then challenged.

"As a result of all this, I started a series of changes in my department and the way I respond to people in it. We've reversed an unhealthy trend that had been building for a long time. I won't say that nobody moonlights any more—I know they do—but the magnitude is much less. Just enough to keep me on my toes. It's only a symptom, not a disease. The way we ran our department was the disease."

I told him that I thought he was still taking it too personally. "Not really," he replied. "I'm the manager, and it's my job to take responsibility for this type of thing. We did have one guy who finally left of his own accord to work full-time in his small computer business. For a few days, I took his leaving as a personal failure, but

I do that whenever anybody leaves. When I reflect upon it, though, I know that a company can't be all things to all people. I think this guy is really happy in his small business in a way he never could have been happy here. Not everybody is destined to be a programmer in a multinational company."

I can't improve on that closing line.

Productivity Measurement: We've Probably Got It Backwards

As any programmer knows from helping other programmers debug, there are worlds to be gained from examining the unexamined assumptions we're inclined to make.

In the States, it's a common word-play to point out that "assume" makes an "ass-" of "-u-" and "-me." Whenever someone comes to us with a program and states, "You needn't look there. I *know* that part's right," we know precisely where to look for the problem.

But it's not only on this small scale that our lives are dictated by unexamined assumptions. Many of the assumptions we live by are couched in phrases that nobody even considers doubting, yet many of these are not only false, but just the opposite of the truth.

I once heard a radio evangelist repeat the old fire-and-brimstone line "The wages of sin is death." In a flash, it struck me that, contrary to this unexamined statement, the wages of sin is *birth*. Aha! Could we be doing the same thing in programming?

I know from long experience that we have some terribly confusing opposites in our terminology. Take "floating point" and "fixed point"—I always had the darndest time remembering which was which.

Then one day, in the midst of a course, it came in a flash, so I told the attentive students, "You can always remember which is floating point and which is fixed point by the following observation: When the decimal point is *fixed* in the word, so it never moves, that's *floating* point; but when the position *floats* in the word, according to the operations performed and the position in the operands, that's *fixed* point!" From that day to this, I've never had a problem.

Recently, I was discussing the problem of evaluating the work of programmers. One talkative manager volunteered his method: "From my desk, I can see the entrances to the cubicles of all my programmers. All I have to do is see which ones are constantly visiting other cubicles to ask questions."

There was silence in the room as everyone considered the implications of this evaluation technique, then somebody said, "You know, I really think you've got something there. Programming's such a complex business that anyone who thinks he knows all the answers and never looks anything up or goes to ask has got to make more trouble than he's worth."

For the first time in a seminar, the talkative manager seemed at a loss for words. Finally he started sputtering, "Um . . . hmmnh . . . you don't understand. Why, if they don't *know* all the answers, why am I paying them all that money?" There was some heated discussion, but in the end the talkative manager never did question his assumption of the high value of a know-it-all programmer.

Later in the same seminar, we discussed more quantitative measures of programmer productivity. There was a lot of sentiment for counting lines of code produced per day, and most of the argument centered on just what should be counted as a line of code. Eventually, I told them about recent studies that showed an inverse correlation between the length of a coded solution and the quality of that solution, based on Halstead's work in software science.

They were befuddled. "If we can't count lines of code, what can we count?" "Isn't it better to count them, even if they are inversely correlated, than to count nothing at all?"

Before I made a hasty answer to that question, I considered how an old assumption becomes perverted into a new falsehood. "Perhaps," I said, "you could reward programmers for producing *fewer* lines of code per day." They shuddered visibly until I put them out of their misery by continuing the line of reasoning.

"But that would soon become a false assumption, too. Why don't you count as productivity (actually its inverse) the number of days required to produce 1,000 lines of code of constant quality working on a problem of standard difficulty?"

"But we can't measure quality!" "Or difficulty!"

"Oh," I replied, stumped again. Then I remembered the backwards principle. "Then perhaps you should be working on those questions first, rather than on irrelevant questions that happen to be easy to answer."

It was their turn to say "Oh."

Can Humor Be Productive?

When things were pretty bleak in Manchester, England, in 1923, my father, then nineteen, packed up his few possessions and emigrated from his birthplace to the former colonies. Although he eventually lost most of his British accent, he never lost his British sense of humor, which caused him no end of trouble in the United States. He was called a communist by the capitalists and a capitalist by the communists, merely because his jokes were not recognized as jokes.

Having a British father and an extremely American mother (who never understood his jokes, either), I was brought up with a sense of humor that *nobody* understood. I often find myself laughing alone in the theater when everyone else is crying or sleeping. Though I've never been seriously called either a communist or a capitalist, I have been misinterpreted from time to time, especially when I try to write something funny.

Evidently, I slipped when I wrote the preceding essay, because D. A. Martin has taken me to task for advocating lines of code as a measure of programmer productivity. Actually, what I thought I was doing was saying that there's no sense whatsoever in measuring lines of code *unless:* (1) the quality of all pieces of work is constant, and (2) the problems worked on are all of the same difficulty. And, since *nobody* knows how to measure those things, I suggested that perhaps we should be working on those questions first.

If I read Martin's letter correctly (and perhaps I don't see *his* humor), he's agreeing with me but elaborating on what might be involved in those two useful measures. He says:

> A program may be implemented by two different programmers in the same period of time. One program contains 200, and the other program 600, lines of code. Who is the more productive? Halstead's observation that the 200 line solution is likely to have greater "quality" . . . is true, but is nonetheless misleading. Surely "quality" in any meaningful sense is expressed in terms of reliability, maintainability, and performance.

Precisely, except that I can't agree with the word "likely." David Coan, in responding to the same article, speaks of "quality" in terms with which I can be extremely sympathetic. He says that all criteria for programming must somehow be related to the question "Is this program good enough for what it's wanted for?"

This is much like the question we put to every formal technical review: Will this product do the job it's supposed to do? The question can be applied to code or to any other product whose "quality" we want to measure.

I believe that this is the top-level question, one step above the measures that Martin suggests, such as "maintainability." I've always argued for maintainability, even back in the days when people accused me of being ignorant for not knowing that "programs, unlike hardware, don't require maintenance"! (That was at the IBM Bald Peak Programming Conference in 1961.) But there are some programs for which "maintainability" is not part of the "job it's supposed to do."

No, I'm not so foolish as to believe the user who swears that *this* program will be run "only once." But when such a person shows up, I offer two prices for the program: *x* dollars for a program that I will destroy after it has been run once, by me personally; and 3*x* dollars for a program that will be capable of being run *twice,* or perhaps more, by me or somebody else. There's no sense charging people for maintainability if they really don't want it. A program that was built to be maintainable (and thus cost several times as much) when there was no requirement for that feature, is not, to my thinking, a quality program.

In other words, quality is relative to the problem at hand. A Rolls-Royce is generally understood to be a quality car. If I owned one out here in Lincoln, Nebraska, it would not meet my requirements for several reasons:

> It wouldn't fit in my garage.
> I'd have difficulty getting parts and/or service.
> It would likely be stolen or molested because of its uniqueness in these parts.

(But don't be discouraged, if any of you were thinking of sending me a Rolls for my birthday. I can always build a new garage.)

I believe Martin is close to this point of view when he says, later in his letter:

> The major point is this: Lines of code are a measure of the *solution* and not the *problem*. The estimator's objective should be to assess the man-effort days required to solve a given problem resulting in an acceptable level of quality. To do this, he should attempt to quantify the *problem* components, not the *solution* (LOC), as in the latter case—he is inevitably making assumptions about the nature of the "best" solution.

Of course, here he's talking about estimating work, rather than evaluating the performance of the worker. If we were interested in measuring the productivity of the worker, then we would presumably want to compare that worker's actual effort with the effort estimated on the basis of the problem's "difficulty."

Conversely, in actual estimating—rather than in setting standard work units for particular tasks—we would have to take the actual worker's productivity into account. There's no sense making an estimate based on availability of workers more capable than we can assign to the job. Perhaps that's one reason we're often so far wrong in our programming estimates.

The simple fact is, though, that we don't know how to assess the "difficulty" inherent in any meaningful problem. In every useful experiment on programming so far performed, where several programmers or teams worked on the "same" problem, there have been variations of 10:1 or more in performance. Usually 30:1 or 50:1 is a more typical figure. My own conclusion from this is that in many cases the concept of "problem difficulty" makes no sense as a measurement. The difficulty seems to be a relationship between the problem and the approach to solving it.

To be sure, some problems are *statistically* easier than others, most of the time. But is this a useful measure? Think of the problem of finding an error in a program. Our tests have shown that certain implanted errors take fifteen minutes for one person to find, fifteen *hours* for another, fifteen *seconds* for a third. A few more people come in at around fifteen minutes, but then we find people who can't find the error no matter how long they search. This kind of variation hardly forms the basis for estimating, even though the average, and even the typical, figure is around fifteen minutes.

Some authors, reacting to this kind of variability, have suggested that the solution lies in hiring only the "best" programmer —the one who finds the error in fifteen seconds. Or, if that's not possible, they propose weeding out the fifteen-hour person and the one who never finds the error. Although there are some certified incompetents in the programming business, there is no such thing as "the programmer who finds the error in fifteen seconds." The person who takes fifteen seconds on one error winds up taking fifteen minutes on the next, and not finding the third at all!

Having these facts concerning human variability uppermost in my mind whenever I write about programming, I think I remain innocent of Martin's accusation:

> Weinberg's strategy of "problem inversion" sounds like a methodology for lateral thinking. It can result in a seductive oversimplification of a problem. Programmer productivity is not an "irrelevant question" which happens to be easy to answer —it is a central issue to all those in the business of manufacturing Software.

Although I appreciate being called seductive, I believe I've been misread—inverted, in fact. I said the "irrelevant question" was "How many lines of code per day does a programmer produce?" Although it presents some minor difficulties, this question is relatively easy to answer—but, I feel, it is irrelevant. I don't at all equate this question with the question "What is a programmer's productivity?" That was the entire point of my previous essay. The strategy of "problem inversion" is not a method of "lateral thinking," but a preparation for being laughed at when your thinking has been backwards for a long time. By showing how frequently we have been 180 degrees wrong, I had hoped to prepare my readers for the revelation that we're doing it again—in counting lines of code.

But alas, my British/American humour/humor was lost on some readers, like Martin, who I thought were 100 percent in agreement with me. Upon reflection, though, I've come to think it may not be my fault (when is it *ever* the programmer's fault?). Martin, as quality assurance manager of NCR Ltd., must be deeply engaged in this productivity question almost every working day, unlike many DP managers who turn to it in despair only when their world is collapsing around them. As a consequence, his thinking on the question is bound to be more profound and more on target than the thinking of the average DP manager.

Unfortunately, both Martin and the average despairing DP manager, when they think about the productivity problem, are not in the mood for jokes. I can understand that, and I appreciate it. But I can't recommend it as a problem-solving method. If we're too serious about so difficult a problem, we're likely to shrug off "ridiculous" suggestions, such as inverting the problem.

And why are these "ridiculous" suggestions so important? There's nothing mysterious about it. If "sensible" suggestions could have solved the problem of measuring productivity, then both Martin and I, and a few hundred other people, would have solved it years ago. The fact that it remains unsolved bears witness to its inherent difficulty. Or, as I just said, to the inherent difficulty in the methods we're trying to apply.

So when I make jokes about productivity measurements, it doesn't mean that I don't take the problem seriously. All it means is that I think the problem is too difficult, and far too important, to be taken seriously all the time.

Come to think of it, perhaps the best measure of a programmer's ability is not lines of code (LOC) but sense of humour (SOH). We're in a tough business. It's tough to do and it's tough to measure. You might be able to survive without turning out oodles of LOC. But when IMS puts an OC3 SVC on your TSO VDU and IBM says there's no ZAP so you'll need an RPQ, you'd better have a good supply of SOH. Otherwise you'll soon be DOA.

The Order of Maria Theresa

I've taken some hard licks at Paul Watzlawick for his naive suggestion about handling terrorist kidnappings. I'd like to even the balance by developing an insight from the first part of his book *How Real Is Real?* Actually, the first part is much better than the second—perhaps he was in a hurry at the end and didn't have time to criticize his own ideas. Besides, there's a world of difference between a wrong idea and a dull one. As long as an idea generates other ideas, there's hope something good might come out of it. And *How Real Is Real?* is full of stimulating ideas, some right and some wrong.

The idea I wish to discuss is embodied in a medal established in Austria during the reign of Empress Maria Theresa—the Order of Maria Theresa. Watzlawick says of this award:

> It remained Austria's highest military decoration until the end of World War I. . . .
> With refreshing absurdity it was reserved exclusively for officers who turned the tide of battle by taking matters into their own hands and actively disobeying orders. Of

course, if things went wrong, they were not decorated but court-martialed for disobedience.

Not content with mere description of this perceptive award from the world's most famous bureaucracy, Watzlawick goes on to editorialize:

> The Order of Maria Theresa is perhaps the supreme example of an official counterparadox, worthy of a nation whose attitude toward the slings and arrows of outrageous fortune has always been characterized by the motto: The situation is hopeless but not serious.

Perhaps Watzlawick should have left well enough alone. The Order of Maria Theresa is a marvel of bureaucratic invention, but it hardly deserves to be called a paradox, let alone a counterparadox. *Every* successful organization—nation, business, or neighborhood kite club—has rules for breaking its own rules. The only unusual aspect of the Order of Maria Theresa is that the rule was written down and officially recognized.

When Jefferson was drafting the United States Constitution, he naturally wrote an article concerning amendments. But when asked to write something granting the people the right to throw out the Constitution entirely and start afresh, Jefferson refused. He argued—correctly, I think—that the people had that right whether or not it was written in the Constitution. It was a right that superseded any government and any written rules of government. It was, in effect, a tautology, for without the consent of the governed, there is no government. A shadow, perhaps, but no government.

The same is true in any modern bureaucracy. Rules are not made to be broken, but neither are they made to be *not* broken. Rules are made so that the organization operates more effectively. The rule above all other rules is "Do what is necessary to operate effectively." You ultimately get punished for not operating effectively, but not for breaking the rules.

The problem with bureaucracies, it seems to me, is that the obverse side of this coin isn't so shiny. If you obey the rules and things turn out badly, you usually don't get punished. In war, the problem may be easier, because if things turn out badly you may be dead and not have to face the Empress at all. In the **XYZ Pork and Bean Factory**, your life is not usually at risk—even if your customers are taking *their* lives in their hands every time they pick up a fork.

I'd be interested in pursuing the biographies of Maria Theresa winners *after* they won the medal. I know that in the United States —where the Medal of Honor is often given under similar circumstances—many winners wind up, as civilians, trying to get a few cents for their medals in a pawn shop. Even medal winning is a short-lived glory in the best of circumstances.

When I started to write this essay, I hoped to conclude by recommending that each organization install an Order of Maria Theresa to counteract the conformist tendencies that infect even the best-managed organizations. But as my thoughts developed, I realized that medals are not the answer. If you're on top of a large organizational pyramid and want protection from your own mistaken orders, you're going to have to work harder than Maria Theresa.

You can start by ensuring that nobody is punished merely for discussing the merits of a particular order of yours. Even if you don't punish discussion, you'll need a long time to overcome the fears people have learned throughout their long careers in *other* organizations. But the long wait will be worth it, for then you will be relieved of the burden of perfection—a burden no person and no nation can long endure.

You might think your next step would be to encourage people to disobey orders they think are wrong or foolish, but they won't need any encouragement if the climate for talking is right. At least some of them won't, and the others will be watching to see what happens to the pioneers. So your second problem comes when someone disobeys—and fails! Now you have the perfect opportunity to play "I told you so," but if you do that, there won't be any further games. Instead, you must get the person to tell you why the order was disobeyed. It might have been a stupid order that would have failed even if it had been carried out. Or it might have been misunderstood—a most likely alternative.

And once you've understood the reasons for the disobedience, drop the whole matter! Everyone is entitled to make a mistake now and then. If people never make mistakes, it means they're never trying and never thinking, which is the most horrible fate a bureaucracy can contemplate. Only if the same person disobeys orders over and over will you have to take any action—and by then your course of action should be obvious.

But won't the repeated failures create a disaster? Perhaps, but then you can take comfort from the Austrian motto: The situation is hopeless but not serious.

In the programming business, we have the comfort of a large cushion of safety in what we do. We make many mistakes, but we have procedures designed to detect them and remove them before they cause too much harm. If those procedures are working well, it gives us some breathing room in which to make mistakes—the same room we need in order to learn. In a situation like that, we shouldn't need medals to keep us disobeying foolish orders.

The Phox and the Pheasants: A Phable

One fine day, a fox moved into the pheasant neighborhood. As the pheasants stood at a distance and watched the van being unloaded, one of them remarked, "A phine thing this is, a phox moving in right next door."

"Indeed," one of the others agreed. "No pheasant in the phlock will be safe, as long as that phox is there."

"No need to be aphraid," said Philip, the youngest. "As long as we stay together, there isn't a phox in the world who could harm us. I think we should call a meeting, to see if we can present a united phront to the phox."

Although they were reluctant to follow the lead of such a young pheasant, the older members of the flock couldn't really deny the wisdom of what he had proposed, so a meeting was called for that very night. At the meeting, agreement was universal that the fox had to be warned in no uncertain terms that pheasant-under-glass was strictly off the menu, unless he wanted to be fox-under-ground. But then the question arose as to *how* he would be told. Philip proposed that a roll-call vote be taken and attached to the resolution of the pheasant assembly, so that the fox could see precisely who had voted to back it up.

"You see," he explained to the assembly, "we have to stand up and be counted, so the phox knows that we are not aphraid. Otherwise he will pick us off one at a time, and make a phancy pheast of us."

But the older pheasants were not convinced. As one of them said, "The phlowery phrases of youth are just phine, but give me the wisdom of age every time." In this instance, the wisdom of age said that the fox was likely to be angered by individual names and caused to act irrationally toward those who had signed. "Better," he argued, "to avoid phace-to-phace conphrontations. A simple show-of-wings vote will carry the phull weight of this assembly. Iph our young pheathered-phriend wants to phace the phox, I move that he be designated to deliver the resolution."

The motion and the resolution carried, but without a roll call, in spite of a final plea by the young pheasant for the others to stand up and be counted. As he carried the resolution to the fox, he knew that he had been given this dangerous job as a punishment for having challenged the wisdom and courage of the elders. "Of course I'm aphraid," he said to himself as he knocked on the front door of the fox, "but I'm phully prepared to phight phor my phreedom."

The fox opened the door and was truly surprised to see his visitor. "My goodness," he cried, "is this a fantom or is it really a feasant come to visit?"

"My name is Philip," said the visitor, ignoring his host's strange accent. "I've been sent by the pheasant assembly to phind you and to deliver this resolution to you, so that we can be good neighbors based on mutual understanding."

"And my name's Freddy," said the fox. "Won't you come in while I read this resolution of yours, so I can give you a reply? Why don't you just sit there by the fonograf?"

While Philip sat trying to conceal his trembling, Freddy read the resolution. When he finished, he said, "Well, Filip, it's full of fine frases, but why didn't the individual members sign it?"

"I can't really say, Phreddy," Philip replied, but Freddy knew why. He could see that if the members of the pheasant assembly were afraid to have their names brought to his attention individually, they would not, in fact, raise any opposition if and when he picked up one of their members for a snack now and then. All except Philip, that is, for this young pheasant, though he was obviously afraid, would fight if attacked. In the final analysis, Freddy had no desire to get pecked about the eyes, especially when there were obviously such easy pickings around.

And so, life in the pheasant neighborhood settled down to what Philip called "phiphty phrightened pheasants and one phat phox."

MORAL: Better to stand up and be counted than to lie down and be eaten.

IN OTHER WORDS: It's not unprofessional to be afraid. It is unprofessional to be a coward.

Part VII

Where Is the Programming Profession Going Next?

What Will Programming
Be Like in One Hundred Years?

Like most people, I'm curious about the future.
Also like many people, I'm *not* very curious about
the past. But as my curiosity about the future has
grown, I've been forced to get acquainted with
history: I'm unable to think of any other way to
satisfy my curiosity about the future than by
studying the past—the time when the present was
still in the future.

Here's an example of what I mean. A friend
of mine showed me a book dated 1884, found in
the attic of a farmhouse near Prairie Home, Nebraska. The book was devoted to the subject of
employment for women. The introduction spoke
generally about the New Age, in which women
were leaving their traditional roles as homemak-
ers—a change that would "surely never be reversed."

The bulk of the book described the most
promising jobs for women, devoting an entire
chapter to each of the most important, such as
medicine. Curiously, the job of secretary wasn't
prominently mentioned. It was called "amanuensis" then, and a business office wasn't considered
a suitable environment for women.

Of course, the typewriter changed all that,

didn't it? Well, not right away, for when the typewriter was introduced, it was naturally operated by men. Only men could work with machines—the assumption ran so deep that in the book no "mechanical" jobs were mentioned. And, of course, only men were amanuenses.

Two of the major jobs caught my attention. The first was the promising profession of picture tinter, a job created by the burgeoning technology of photography. Photography was growing so popular that studios couldn't keep up with the demand for young ladies to tint photographs. Anyone with an artistic bent could learn this profession and thus be assured of lifelong employment.

The other promising new profession was telegraph operator. This high-technology job did involve machinery, but the author took great pains to point out that modern inventions had simplified the task of using the telegraph machines. In recent trials, ladies had often proved as adept as gentlemen at using the coding key.

Of course, if the author had been more aware of the technical developments of her time, she might not have made such glowing promises about careers in telegraphy. Most likely, though, she would have interpreted these developments as one Western Union official had done ten years earlier when experiments showed the possibility of transmitting human voices directly by wire. A *Scientific American* article quoted this official as saying (in 1874) that the new discoveries had taken

> the first step toward doing away with manipulating instruments (i.e., telegraph keys) altogether. . . . In time, the operators will transmit the sound of their own voices over the wire, and talk with one another instead of telegraphing.

Our author, had she been a proper futurist, should have told the young ladies to prepare for their future as telegraphers by taking voice training! That would have been considered a shocking and daring futuristic prediction. Still, it might ultimately have been accepted as profound advice.

But suppose she or the Western Union official had hinted that almost everyone would have a telephone *at home*. Even worse, suppose they had predicted that the telephone in each home would be used without the presence of a skilled operator? Nobody would have believed them, and they would have been shunned into the land of forgotten futurists.

And rightly shunned! Why? Because people don't really want to know what one hundred years in the future, or even fifty, will be like. They want to know where they can get a job next week or where they can invest their money until next year. They didn't want to know about the future in 1884, and they won't in 1984. And I'll stick my neck out and predict that they won't in 2084, either.

Actually, it's extremely easy to predict the future. Here are some laws you will need to apply:

1. In the short run, some things will be pretty much the same as they are now.
2. In the long run, some things will be so different than they are now that there's no way to predict them.
3. In the long run, though, we'll all be dead, so we certainly won't be interested in what someone predicted one hundred years earlier, right or wrong.
4. We all do our living in the short run, some a bit shorter than others, but short all the same.

These laws allow you to make long-run predictions in any way you like. For instance, I predict that in 2084 the concept of "computer" won't exist, except as an archaic word like "amanuensis." Instead of computers, we'll have "emoters." Emoters will be semi-living, manufactured biological systems that eliminate problems by making us not worry about them rather than by "solving" them in the present sense of that word.

Naturally there won't be any more programmers. They will have gone the way of the photo tinters. (Yes, I know there are a few people tinting photographs today to create that old-fashioned look. There probably will be a few PASCAL programmers working in theme parks—we'll surely still have some theme parks, won't we?)

Instead of programmers, we'll have "swimmers." Their job will be to enter into communion with the emoters by submerging themselves in the giant vats of safflower oil in which emoters work and by rubbing themselves all over the emoters' bodies. (Oh, yes, I can hear some of you saying, "What about *distributed* emoters? Remember the telephone?" But traveling to the emoter vats will be a religious pilgrimage, so nobody would want to have their own personal emoter at home. Besides, emoters will smell awful.)

Gee, this predicting business is fun! I could go on for pages—but you wouldn't be interested. Because you, like me, do your living in the short run.

You *would* be interested if you didn't want to think about your own short-run prospects. That's why I read science fiction on twenty-seven-hour flights to Australia. But if you're thinking about your professional future as a programmer, you won't be pleased if I advise you to learn to swim in safflower oil.

Well, what can I tell you for the more immediate future—for, say, your professional life? Here are a few ideas:

1. Although things may extrapolate linearly in the short run, you can forget about those extrapolations that say that at present rates there will be 500 million programmers in the United States by the year 2015.

2. Indeed, because of such extrapolations, frightened entrepreneurs are financing ways of cutting down the need for programmers. The same thing happened with telephone operators. With operator assistance on every call, our present rate of calling would require everyone in the United States to be a telephone operator—and then who would make the calls? The fact is we wouldn't even have the present telephone system unless some way had been found to reduce the number of operators per call.

3. The same kind of thing *must* happen in programming, if present trends continue. Some of the methods of reducing programming needs will pay off, though it is hard to say with certainty which ones. But notice that there are still more telephone operators today than there were fifty years ago, and lots more than there were one hundred years ago.

4. There are still a few 1401 Autocoder jobs available today, and twenty years from now there will probably be more 360/370 Assembler and COBOL jobs. You may not want these jobs, however.

There are other predictions I could make, but I think the message is clear. There will be programming jobs aplenty throughout your professional life, but the ones you'll be most interested in will probably be very different from the programming job you now have. To prepare for such a future, you'll have to prepare for change.

How does one prepare for change? I'll have more to say about that elsewhere, but as long as we're on the level of sweeping generalities, here's one more:

5. No matter where we look in history, we never find anyone who lived more than one day at a time. We do sometimes find people who lived *less*.

Who were these people who lived less than one day at a time? Most of them were people who, instead of living, dreamed about living in the future. The way to prepare for living in the future is to live fully in the present!

So don't ask "What will programming be like in one hundred years?" Instead, take a look at what you're doing *now*. Ask yourself, "What have I learned today?" If the answer is "little or nothing," then your future as a professional programmer is not much brighter than your present. Could that be why your dreams are projected into the unreachable future?

How Long Should a Programming Career Be?

In its crudest form, typological thinking imagines that there is some reality to the "average" individual. For example, suppose we surveyed the audience attending the ballet at a Saturday matinee. It happens to be sold out to the local Masonic temple whose members are taking their young daughters for a bit of culture. In such an audience, we might have 5-year-old girls about 3 feet tall and weighing 50 pounds, plus an equal number of 35-year-old men about 6 feet tall and weighing 200 pounds. From such a survey, we could easily conclude that the "typical" aficionado of the ballet was a 20-year-old fat midget, four-feet-six tall and weighing 125 pounds—and a hermaphrodite, to boot.

—Weinberg and Weinberg/*On the Design of Stable Systems,* p. 56

Much typological nonsense has been written on the subject of "programmer burnout." This supposed phenomenon is characterized by a relationship between productivity and experience indicated in Figure 4.

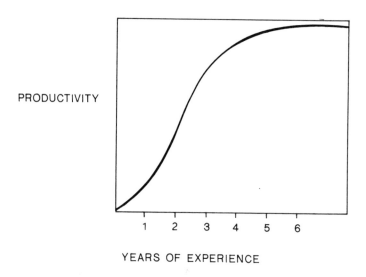

PRODUCTIVITY

1 2 3 4 5 6

YEARS OF EXPERIENCE

Figure 4. How Productivity Seems to Correlate with Years of Experience

According to this picture, after three years, additional years of experience don't seem to add significantly to a programmer's productivity. Managers who hold to this model naturally are unwilling to pay a premium for many years of experience. Usually, they will seek programmers in the job market with one or two years of experience.

One problem with this model is that it may fail to consider problem difficulty. In most shops, the more experienced programmers are given, on the average, more difficult programs to write. If the measures of productivity fail to consider problem difficulty, the more experienced programmers will naturally have their productivity underestimated. In some cases, a more realistic model would be that of Figure 5.

This slightly less pessimistic curve is supported by the results of a number of studies in the psychology of programming. When programmers of varying experience are asked to perform the same task—coding, finding bugs, developing test data—the average performance versus experience curve frequently looks like that of Figure 5. Even so, a manager studying Figure 5 may still wish to

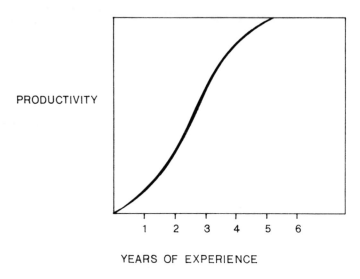

PRODUCTIVITY

YEARS OF EXPERIENCE

Figure 5. The Productivity/Experience Curve Corrected for Problem Difficulty

follow the strategy of hiring programmers with very little experience in order to take advantage of the steeply rising segment of the curve. Conversely, programmers often tolerate low-paying jobs in their first year or two in order to be in a firm that pays well for longevity rather than for actual output.

Both Figures 4 and 5 represent models of the average programmer. In really large firms, employing hundreds or thousands of programmers, personnel policies may force managers to follow the averages in hiring and setting wages. In smaller firms, however, they may have more discretion. If they are perceptive, they can profit by noting the difference between each individual programmer and the presumed average.

The same studies of programming that produced **Figure 5** support the view that a manager does well by appraising the *quality* of each candidate's experience. Does the programmer really have ten years of experience, or is it more accurately characterized as one year of experience, ten times? If we divide the programmers in each study into two groups—high performance and low performance—we generally find that the experience curves look like those in Figure 6.

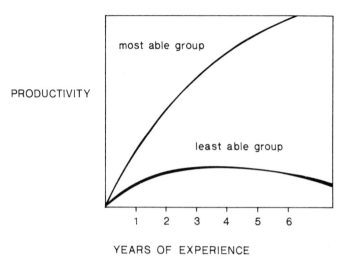

Figure 6. The Productivity/Experience Curve Seen as a Composite

The curve we see in Figure 4 or Figure 5 is probably a mixing of these two curves into a single curve.

Do these two curves represent anything real, or are they artificial manipulations of data? My own experience with such studies and on the job tells me there is an important truth here. To understand it, pretend we are able to follow the careers of one hundred programmer trainees who started together six years ago. Each year, some of them will drop out of programming because they don't like it or can't do it very well. These dropouts will be high at the beginning, then decline as salaries rise to overcome any residual job dissatisfaction.

After a year or two, some of the better performers will be offered promotions outside of programming. Some will accept. Some will decline, preferring the work they like and do well. Generally, though, the promotions will be offered principally to those who are the better programmers—whether or not they are the most qualified to be analysts, managers, or data-base administrators.

The following table shows how the allocation of these hypothetical one hundred trainees might evolve over a six-year period:

Year	Number remaining in programming	Number dropped out (cumulative)	Number promoted out (cumulative)
0	100	0	0
1	85	15	0
2	75	20	5
3	65	20	15
4	45	20	35
5	35	20	45
6	30	20	50

The figures are not meant to be exact, but only suggestive of trends.

Now suppose we break down this table into two tables, each starting with fifty of the trainees. First, we have the "least able" fifty:

Year	Number in programming	Number dropped out	Number promoted out
0	50	0	0
1	37	13	0
2	32	17	1
3	30	17	3
4	26	17	7
5	24	17	9
6	23	17	10

Now consider the "most able" fifty:

Year	Number in programming	Number dropped out	Number promoted out
0	50	0	0
1	48	2	0
2	43	3	4
3	35	3	12
4	19	3	28
5	11	3	36
6	7	3	40

In other words, according to this model, after six years about 77 percent of the thirty remaining programmers come from the 50 percent lowest in ability. The very worst have dropped out early. On the other hand, most of the better ones have been promoted out to meet rapidly growing demands for experienced personnel in non-programming jobs.

The same kind of modeling can be applied if we assume that the programmers' original ability is not the only or most crucial factor. Whatever factors we consider, we have to avoid assuming that the population we see is somehow static. That assumption leads to typological fallacies.

What you see in a population is a result of many selective forces, so it's easy to think you are measuring one thing when you're really measuring a combination of two or more factors. For instance, instead of measuring years of experience, we may actually be measuring a combination of years passed over for promotion and years refused to take a promotion.

It's harmful when management makes this kind of typological mistake, but it's usually not fatal. But when an individual makes the same mistake, it can lead to personal tragedy. Instead of believing typological mythology, the individual will want to base personal choices on actual *persons*.

Do you have to burn out after three years? Don't look at the "average" programmer! See if you can find a ten-year veteran who's still going strong. Then find out what makes that person tick. Find a few other people and model yourself after the best in each of them. Whatever you do, don't model yourself on the average—unless you're a fat hermaphroditic midget!

How Long Should I Stay in Programming?

After I wrote about typological thinking applied to the question of the length and productivity of a programming career, several correspondents were happy to see the fallacy of the "three-year burnout" exposed, but they expressed dissatisfaction with the essay. As one observed, "You never really answered the question in the title: How long should a programming career be?"

I didn't answer because I didn't know. Or, rather, I didn't know how to answer such a general, sociological question. I'm a lot more comfortable with personal, anecdotal thinking, so I'd prefer to rephrase the question: How long should I stay in programming?

A question like that gets me thinking in terms of specifics. If I let my mind wallow in specifics, something usually emerges, after which I can clean it up, polish it, and package it as a general principle.

For some reason I didn't appreciate at the time, this programming question reminded me of my reading compulsion. I must have acquired this habit early, for I recall reading cereal boxes at breakfast when I was four years old. My greatest fear when traveling was to be stranded in an airport after the bookstore had closed. Recently, however, I overcame my fear of airports by learning the pleasures of reading telephone directories.

I believe my interest in phone directories started in Iceland. Because of its size and isolation, Iceland contains a mixture of past and future that is sure to delight American and European travelers. For instance, the entire capital was heated by geothermal energy— and still is—long before *geothermal* became chic.

Iceland also has a modern phone system, including a directory, but the directory contains a few surprises from the past. If you want to look up somebody in the directory, you quickly discover that the names are arranged alphabetically—but by first name!

Until the fourteenth century, few people in Europe had last names. As population grew larger, more urban, and more mobile, first names were no longer adequate for bureaucratic purposes. In Iceland, however, the modernization has been slow, and the system from our own European past has been retained.

When family names were adopted, several different systems were used. In northern areas, such as Iceland, two people with the same name were commonly distinguished by referring to the father's name. For classifying by family name, this system was made permanent, for the bureaucracy couldn't tolerate changing each generation from Olaf Jonson to Sigmund Olafson to Ivar Sigmundson. (Don't ask me why bureaucracies can tolerate the change in women's names with marriage.)

In Iceland, the system hasn't been made permanent. Father's name is listed in the directory, but it's not the basis for alphabetical order. Why should it be? It's only used to distinguish between identical first names. Occupation is also used as another aid in distinguishing between people in the directory, just as it was used before last names were generally adopted.

We have hundreds of occupation names in the United States directories, even though we rarely think about their source. For many names, such as Smith and Fuller, the original occupation has all but disappeared. I noticed in the Lincoln phone book that there is a Waggoner Auto Repair. I wonder if the Waggoners ever think about the origin of their family name. Perhaps their family simply converted from wagon work to auto work as they passed the trade down from generation to generation.

Some people argue that programming won't last long enough to become hereditary. I've never found a Programmer in a directory, though I have found quite a few Coders. Has coding seen its peak, now to go the way of blacksmithing?

As people stopped using horses, they naturally didn't need as many blacksmiths, and the name Smith became something of a feeble echo. Programs are today's workhorses, though programmers may not have to worry just yet about enduring the fate of the Smiths.

But that wasn't the only fate of traditional trades. The population has grown since the Middle Ages, and we still consume generous quantities of flour. So what has happened to the Miller who used to inhabit every little village? Each of us uses thousands of times more candlepower than our ancestors. So where are the thousands of times more Chandlers?

The case of the Chandlers is an instructive parallel to programming. It is because we now use so much light that we can no longer depend on candles. Cheap light led to increased demand, and increased demand led to cheaper light.

In the same way, the market for programming will depend on the cost of programming. If the cost goes too high, the market may decline. Or, more likely, the market will begin to look for cheaper substitutes.

In the traditional occupations, these changes often took more than a lifetime and frequently they spanned generations. In programming, we've already seen many such changes within one lifetime, a situation that's bound to cause great stress on the individual, just as the former changes caused stress on families.

Many programmers have reacted to the stress of change by personally avoiding change, either by finding a job where "traditional" methods are still used or by abandoning programming for some nontechnical work like management or administration.

There must be some very strong force within human beings that makes them hang on to trades generation after generation. Changing one's work may well be more difficult than suggested by the prophets who predict an impending technological utopia. For one thing, it may involve loss of personal identity, just as it formerly meant loss of family identity. On the other hand, perhaps this loss is a small price to pay for "progress."

The three-years-and-out career is based on a fallacy. Worse than that, it's a self-fulfilling prophecy. If you believe it, you stop trying to improve and start thinking about how to escape to some other line of work.

Perhaps it's time to probe the underlying human processes that determine how long people stay in programming and how the image of a "proper" career affects their work as programmers. As a first approximation, we should consider the balance between (1) stagnation when people feel they're secure, whether they learn anything or not, and (2) stagnation when people feel they aren't going to be in the trade long enough to bother learning anything.

The first tendency is evident among university professors, especially those who have tenure. The second is especially widespread among programmers. Yet there are many professors and programmers who continually renew themselves. How are they different from the others?

If we can answer that, we can answer the question of how long one should remain in programming. First we change the question to this form: How do I know when it's time to quit programming?

The answer to that one is easy. I call it the Professional Expiration Test: When learning's finished, *you're* finished!

Which brings me full circle, back to reading telephone directories. If you can make something useful out of "lost" time in airports, surely you can make something useful out of "lost" time in a university or programming job. If not, you haven't got the compulsion and it's time to escape.

How Can I Prepare Myself for the Future?

"Would you tell me, please, which way I ought to go from here?"

"That depends a good deal on where you want to get to," said the Cat.

"I don't much care where—" said Alice.

"Then it doesn't much matter which way you go," said the Cat.

"—so long as I get *somewhere*," Alice added as an explanation.

"Oh, you're sure to do that," said the Cat, "if you only walk long enough."

—Lewis Carroll/*Alice's Adventures in Wonderland*

The computer business over the past few decades has been so dynamic that anyone who started walking early enough was almost sure to get *somewhere*. Although opportunities are still very great today, the would-be professional might be able to use a bit more direction than the Cheshire Cat was able to give Alice.

Fortunately for Alice, a proper upbringing had prepared her for her adventures in Wonderland. Whatever peculiar problem Alice chanced to encounter, she could draw upon general principles to save the day—or at least to keep her out of too much trouble.

For instance, right after she tumbled down the rabbit hole, she was faced with that peculiar little bottle with the tag reading "Drink me." Undismayed, Alice worked out the proper course of behavior:

> It was all very well to say "Drink me," but the wise little Alice was not going to do *that* in a hurry. "No, I'll look first," she said, "and see whether it's marked 'poison' or not"; for she had read several nice little stories about children who had got burnt, and eaten up by wild beasts, and other unpleasant things, all because they *would* not remember the simple rules their friends had taught them: such as, that a red-hot poker will burn you if you hold it too long; and that, if you cut your finger *very* deeply with a knife, it usually bleeds; and she had never forgotten that, if you drink much from a bottle marked "poison," it is almost certain to disagree with you, sooner or later.

Alice's rules would certainly be useful to those of us seeking adventures in Programmingland: Don't hold red-hot pokers too long; don't cut yourself too deeply with a knife; and don't drink too much from a bottle marked "poison." Even though the future is a cloudy glass, we can certainly make some extrapolation from observing that, in the past,

1. No programmer has ever suffered too much from being in good health.

It may seem unnecessary to remind you of this, but many professional programmers are like little children with red-hot pokers when it comes to their own bodies. So if you want to "get somewhere" in programming, your luck will be greatly enhanced if you manage to find some way to stay healthy. Or to get healthy, if you're not right now!

What other words of wisdom can we glean from the past? Thinking over the many professionals I've known, I can fairly say that

2. No programmer's career was ever severely retarded by an excess of self-knowledge.

That's not to say that you can't get ahead in programming *without* self-knowledge. If that were true, I wouldn't be here writing this. My early career was characterized by personal blind spots broad enough to eclipse the Milky Way. I wish I could say that my later career was blessed with greater insight, but it seems that the more I've learned the less I know about myself. I do now see how my early chances would have been improved had I occasionally been able to get outside myself. How many barrels of midnight oil I've wasted over problems that rested squarely behind one of my blind spots!

I had always been adept at noticing the blind spots of other people. When I eventually began to realize the extent of my own blindness, I noticed that other people were talented at seeing what I couldn't see. This led me to seek the help of others' eyes, in exchange for my helping them with mine.

Getting and giving this kind of personal vision wasn't always as easy as I expected it to be, but it taught me another great lesson:

3. No programmer has ever been seriously hindered by an ability to get along with other people.

Notice that I said "get along," not "go along." It's a fine distinction, but one the computer forces us to make. The computer never "goes along." Some people are infuriated by this "straight-arrow" behavior, but such people don't last as programmers. Eventually, professionals come to realize that the computer doesn't tell lies to win its point—because its point is simple fact. Nor does it try to manipulate you to get its way—because it has no way.

People learn to be straight with computers because the computer is straight with them. People learn to be crooked in response to crooked systems, which leads to three more principles for success:

4. No programmer has ever been maimed by being straight with a computer or with straight-dealing people.
5. Many programmers have been hurt by trying to deal straight with bent people, but they've all recovered.

6. Many programmers have been bent by trying to deal crooked with bent people, and often the bending is permanent and crippling.

I guess it all comes down to being *skilled at disagreement* and *willing to endure hardship* for limited periods. It helps if your job is not on the line, or if you have alternatives:

7. No programmer ever backed down from a professional stance because there was money in the personal bank account or a job offer in the wings.

But it also helps if you understand that problems aren't merely problems, but *opportunities for learning.* Leaving a job is a way of avoiding a mess of trouble, but

8. No programmer ever got into a mess of trouble that didn't offer several opportunities for increasing self-knowledge and the ability to get along successfully with other people.

If you don't believe this, you need only read what happened to Alice, or to any of the thousands of other protagonists of literary adventures.

My own adventures in Programmingland have taught me that the secret of preparing for an uncertain future is not in learning new COBOL verbs, but rather in acquiring new problem-solving skills of broad application. My own work as a consultant has taken this turn, heavily influenced by the work of Carl Rogers. In his book *On Personal Power,* Rogers explains:

> The individual and not the problem is the focus. The aim is not to solve one particular problem but to assist the individual to *grow,* so he can cope with the present problem and with later problems in a better integrated fashion.

Which leads to my final principle:

9. No programmer who continues to grow need fear the future.

The Tortoise and the Hair: A Fable

One autumn evening, an old tortoise was enjoying the sunset on his front porch, reminiscing about his greatest victories of the past, and listening to an exquisite Mozart Horn Concerto on the stereo. All of a sudden, his reveries were brusquely interrupted by the sound of a young hare rumbling by on his motorcycle, listening to a rock group on his transistor. After the hare had passed down his street a second time, the tortoise had had enough.

"Hey there, you young whippersnapper," he called out, "why don't you turn off that 'yeh-yeh' and listen to something quiet and cultivated?"

The hare screeched his bike to a stop in front of the tortoise's porch. "Look here, Pops," he answered, trying to be as respectful as possible. "I'm not telling you what to listen to, so why should you tell me? Besides, you're the 'snapper,' not me. I'm a hare, not a tortoise."

"I'll say you're a hair," snapped the tortoise, who was becoming a bit hard of hearing. "Just look at you; you're *covered* with hair. Why can't you keep your hair to a respectable length, as I do?"

"Look, Mister Tortoise, I'm trying to explain. I have this hair because I'm a hare. You're bald as a tortoise because you're a tortoise. But I'm not torturing you to go out and grow some hair, so why not pay me the same service?"

But the tortoise was rather sensitive about his hairless shell, so he switched topics. "And another thing—that motorcycle! Why can't you drive a car, like any respectable citizen?"

"I can't afford a car."

"That's poppycock," the tortoise admonished. "In the first place, if you'd get a job and do some honest work, you *could* afford it . . ."

"But I have a job, only it doesn't pay much . . ."

". . . and in the second place," said the tortoise, who did not like to be contradicted, "you only want that machine so you can go racing around the highways killing innocent bystanders. Well, I'll show you a thing or two. When I was your age, I was road-racing champion of the state. Beat your own grandfather, I did! It was written up in all the papers. Now you get on your little motorcycle, because I'm going to get out my car and have you a *real* race, not a children's game!"

"Hey, Pops," called the hare to the departing tortoise, "I don't want to race you. Grandpa told me you used to be the hottest driver in these parts, and I believe him. But you're a little old for that kind of thing now . . ."

But that was exactly the wrong thing to say and only served to further enrage the tortoise, who was by this time already racing down the driveway. Unfortunately, his eyesight was not what it used to be, especially since he didn't like to be seen in public with his tortoise-shell glasses. As he roared out into the street, he crashed broadside into a police cruiser that had just pulled up to tell the hare not to be loitering around this nice neighborhood with his motorcycle. Though nobody was injured, the tortoise's car was a total wreck—which didn't matter very much to him, since his driver's license was revoked for driving without his glasses.

MORAL: No matter how impetuous youth may be, no matter how noisy, how uncultivated, how poor or long of hair, in the end, age always loses.

IN OTHER WORDS: The ultimate act of a professional is a gracious retirement.

Epilogue

An epilogue is "a short addition or concluding section at the end of any literary work, often dealing with the future of its characters." This book may or may not be literary, and it has but one character—the professional programmer. Besides that, you've probably just finished reading about the future. So why have an epilogue at all?

I'm not really sure of the answer to that question, but there are several possibilities:

1. My editor yells at me when I don't end with sufficient drama.
2. Some readers can be thwarted when they try to read the last part of the book first, possibly to avoid reading the entire boring mess.
3. I feel somehow that there's more to be said.

None of these is a particularly good reason for writing an epilogue, though perhaps taken together they sum up to one passable reason. There must be something stronger driving me, which for some reason is related to the following story.

The great professor of astronomy was wakened in the middle of the night by a loud pounding on his front door. When he stuck his head out the bedroom window he saw that the source of the noise was a young man who was a student in his course on the evolution of the universe.

"What do you want at this hour of the night?" the professor complained.

"I'm sorry to waken you, sir, but I've been terribly depressed and agitated. I can't sleep, and I'm afraid I might do myself some injury."

"I'm sorry to hear that, but what can that have to do with me?"

"It's because of your lecture," the student explained. "All that talk about the end of the universe has upset me something awful."

"I hardly think you need to be upset," the professor chided him. "After all, I told you that the end of the universe wouldn't come for 100 billion years!"

"Oh! I thought you said 100 million!"

Now why should that story come to my mind when I'm writing an epilogue to a book for and about the professional programmer? I've had the experience, more than once, of being awakened in the middle of the night for some "emergency" that proved no more urgent than this student's plea. I think that many professional programmers have had the same experience, as well as other experiences that could easily make them overestimate the importance of what they're doing.

The programming business has been a good one over the past few decades. In the next few, it promises to be just as good, perhaps better. Anyone with a bent for programming is living in a lucky time, but that's really all it is—luck. Fifty years ago, our services weren't worth a nickel, and fifty years from now it might be worse. I wouldn't be surprised in fifty years to learn that programmers were being hanged.

But your own worth as a person is not much related to your worth as a labor commodity. After all, of what use is a baby? Because you're well paid and much sought after, you could easily forget about your worthy qualities other than your skill as a programmer. Should our business ever take a tumble, you'd be in for a cracking that would make Humpty Dumpty seem hard-boiled.

I saw this happen to some of my friends in the early 1970s. It wasn't pretty, and it could happen again. The ones who were hurt most were the ones who had been riding highest—not the ones who necessarily had the best jobs, but the ones who had somehow blown themselves up all out of proportion.

But it could actually be worse if things *never* crash for you. Your self-image will keep inflating until, at last, you'll be an insufferable, pompous bore to all your family, friends, and neighbors. I know that's what happens to me whenever one of my books is well received, and I know how hard it is for my friends who attempt to bring me back to earth.

So I worry what I might be doing by writing an entire book about the professional programmer, what I might be adding to an inflated feeling of self-importance that some programmers already possess. If they're like me, that feeling can generate much unhappiness—a feeling that *my* problems are bigger, more important, and harder to solve than the problems of ordinary people.

Next time you're feeling that way, try thinking of the astronomy student and the 100 million or 100 billion years left. Or think of the 5 billion other people now living on this planet. Or of the 100 billion galaxies in the universe, each with perhaps 1 trillion stars, each of which could well have another 5 billion "people" attached to them.

Many of those "people" are probably programmers, and a few billion of them are probably experiencing the same bugs you are, right at this very moment. When I'm stuck on something, I find this thought of astronomic companionship most comforting. And that's what I wanted to tell you, as an epilogue to this book: *You'll sleep much better if you have a reasonable perspective on your place in the universe.*

A Professional Bibliography

It's a great thing to start life with a small number of really good books which are your very own.

—Sir Arthur Conan Doyle

The serious programmer should certainly start professional life with a "small number of really good books." Unfortunately, the number of really good books in programming is very small to begin with, while at the same time the number of not-so-good, but essential, books—such as reference manuals—is always increasing. Then, too, there never seems to be enough time for reading.

Speed-reading may help, but I have my own system that's even faster. I try hard to read only the very best books, and to give them my utmost attention. This tactic also raises my level of reading enjoyment, building up an emotional reserve for those books I must read that may not be so nicely written.

The following is an annotated, highly selective list of books that have influenced my image of what a professional programmer might achieve and how that achievement might be realized.

Few of the books on the list have any direct connection with programming, but don't let that worry you. Programmers may be unique, but they are, so far, still part of the human race.

Boulding, Kenneth. *The Image: Knowledge in Life and Society.* Ann Arbor: University of Michigan Press, 1956.

This classic essay is required reading for anyone who is concerned about the shaping of new professionals and a new profession. Your thinking process will never be the same after you've absorbed the message of this prize-winning book.

Kennedy, Eugene. *On Becoming a Counselor.* New York: Continuum Publishing Corp., 1980.

This book says not a single word about computer programming, but it says many words about being a professional in the service of other people. The intelligent reader won't have any trouble knowing which parts to skip. I think it might be better to read the Carl Rogers book *On Personal Power* before reading this one. But if you're considering an offer to leave technical work or to take a supervisory status, it will be well worth your time to read both of these books before making a decision.

Kernighan, Brian W., and P. J. Plauger. *The Elements of Programming Style.* New York: McGraw-Hill, 1974.

This is a little book and not hard to read, but full of subtle lessons for the working programmer. In the first week after you read it, you'll earn back the few hours consumed in the reading by avoiding some nasty problem in your work. The author's other work, *Software Tools,* is also a worthwhile addition to your bookshelf, but read it after you've read this classic.

Knuth, Donald E. *The Art of Computer Programming, vol. 3, Sorting and Searching.* Reading, Mass.: Addison-Wesley, 1973.

Any of the books in Knuth's ambitious series would sit well on the shelves of the professional programmer, but far too many copies of these prestigious works merely sit on shelves. Perhaps they are too imposing in thickness and density, so I'm recommending only one as a starter. I've chosen this one because it's the one I refer to most and perhaps it is easiest for the largest number of professionals to relate to. The point of Knuth's books, in the present context, is not any particular technical material but, as Knuth puts it, "an ideal framework for discussing a wide variety of general issues," such as "How can a person choose rationally between different algorithms for the same application?" Every hour spent with Knuth will improve the thought processes of the professional programmer.

Linger, Richard C., Harlan D. Mills, and Bernard I. Witt. *Structured Programming: Theory and Practice.* Reading, Mass.: Addison-Wesley, 1979.

If a professional programmer were to read only one book on "structured programming," this should be it. This is not a book to be skimmed, but it's not unnecessarily difficult either. The style and content of this book set the tone for professional programming of the future.

Morrison, Philip, and Emily, eds. *Charles Babbage and His Calculating Engines.* New York: Dover, 1961.

Any professional has to be interested in how it all got started. Babbage was the first real computer professional, and many of his problems are similar to the problems faced by professionals today. Reading about his life and times, his successes and failures, should help to create the kind of perspective every professional needs.

Pye, David. *The Nature and Art of Workmanship.* New York: Van Nostrand Reinhold, 1968.

Every professional programmer should be intensely interested in workmanship, and everyone intensely interested in workmanship should read Pye.

Rogers, Carl. *On Personal Power: Inner Strength and Its Revolutionary Impact.* New York: Dell Publishing Co., 1977.

A book for all those who would like to develop power over their professional life, and over themselves, without developing power over other people. Any programmer who can absorb Rogers into the blood will become twice the professional and ten times the person.

Schneider, Ben Ross, Jr. *Travels in Computerland.* Reading, Mass.: Addison-Wesley, 1974.

This is a view of our business from the outside, by someone who tried to use our services. It may help to keep insiders on an even keel, and it's great fun to read.

Shute, Nevil. *Trustee from the Toolroom*. New York: William Morrow & Co., 1960.

This charming novel was recommended to me by Barbara Walker in response to one of the essays in this book. Any true craftsperson will be delighted with this story of the rewards of dedication to professional work.

Terkel, Studs. *Working*. New York: Avon Books, 1975.

This best-seller is a compendium of personal statements by workers from all sorts of backgrounds in all sorts of jobs. It's fun and moving to read, and is sure to contribute insight into your own attitudes toward work.

Selected Books from the Little, Brown Computer Systems Series

In addition to the above list, I'd like to call your attention to the following books as candidates for your professional library. Because they are all part of the Little, Brown Computer Systems Series, and because I am series editor for that series (as well as author of several of the books), I have a personal stake in their success. Therefore, I cannot be sure that my recommendation is entirely disinterested. I naturally think they are good books, though not necessarily classics such as those listed above, or I wouldn't have accepted them for the series. Ultimately, you'll have to form your own opinion, but I'd like to hear from you about these books so that I can shape the future series in a responsive way.

Freedman, Daniel P., and Gerald M. Weinberg. *Handbook of Walkthroughs, Inspections, and Technical Reviews,* 3rd Ed.

Everything you always wanted to know about how programmers can help each other improve through the technique of formal technical reviews.

Gause, Donald C., and Gerald M. Weinberg. *Are Your Lights On?*

How to know whether you're solving the right problem and solving the problem right.

Mosteller, William. *The Systems Programmer's Problem Solver.*

A compendium of techniques that will be of immediate aid to the systems programmer or to one who aspires to be a systems programmer.

Parikh, Girish. *Techniques of Program and System Maintenance.*

Articles from numerous sources on that taboo subject—maintenance. Most of the articles are sure to be useful to the serious professional programmer.

Shneiderman, Ben. *Software Psychology.*

A collection of what we know about how programming should be carried out, as well as how we know these things.

Weinberg, Gerald M., Stephen E. Wright, Richard Kauffman, and Martin A. Goetz. *High Level COBOL Programming.*

A view of how the COBOL world can be raised to a higher level, taking with it the thousands of COBOL programmers who are ready and willing to grow.

Weinberg, Gerald M. *Rethinking Systems Analysis and Design.*

Another collection of essays similar to *Understanding the Professional Programmer,* that will interest any professional programmer who is involved with design or analysis, or with designers or analysts.

Index